A
PUBLIC
CITIZEN'S
ACTION
MANUAL

An Athenian citizen does not neglect his state because he takes care of his own household; even those of us who are engaged in business have a very fair idea of politics. We do not regard a man who takes no interest in public affairs as harmless. We do not say that such a man "minds his own business." Rather we say he has no business here at all.

—Pericles

As soon as several of the inhabitants of the United States have taken up an opinion or a feeling which they wish to promote in the world, they look around for mutual assistance; and as soon as they have found each other out, they combine. From that moment they are no longer isolated men, but a power seen from afar, whose actions serve for an example, and whose language is listened to.

—Alexis de Tocqueville

A PUBLIC CITIZEN'S ACTION MANUAL

by DONALD K. ROSS

GROSSMAN PUBLISHERS, NEW YORK 1973

First published in 1973 in a hardbound and paperbound edition
by Grossman Publishers, Inc.
625 Madison Avenue, New York, N.Y. 10022

Published simultaneously in Canada by
Fitzhenry and Whiteside, Ltd.

SBN 670–58201–8 (hardbound)
    670–58202–6 (paperbound)

Library of Congress Catalogue Card Number: 72–9904

Printed in U.S.A.

ACKNOWLEDGMENTS

This book could not have been written without the assistance of
many dedicated citizen activists. Sandy Dement Sterling, Ruth
Fort and Sharland Trotter helped with editing. For the consumer
section, special thanks are due Carl Nash, Robert Vaughn, Mark
Frederickson, Ron Landsman, Fairfax Leary, Jr., Kate Blackwell,
Karen Ferguson and Dave Calfee.

Assistance on health projects was received from Susan Kline,
Pat Powers, Andrea Hricko, Sid Wolfe and Gary Grindler.

Members of the New York City feminist law firm of Bellamy,
Blank, Goodman, Kelly, Ross & Stanley helped with the preparation of the equal opportunity projects.

Projects in the tax section were designed and written by Jona-
than Rowe, an attorney for the Tax Reform Research Group
and editor of *People and Taxes*.

Special thanks are due the PIRGs and the Connecticut Citizen
Action Group, who put some of these projects into practice.

Susan Zaro, Susan Perry, Connie Jo Smith, Joan Rowan and
Karen Klinginsmith helped with production of the manuscript.

Introduction

In the early days of the Republic, the federal government did little beyond run the post office, collect tariffs, and provide for the common defense. And the state governments did even less. Instead, the symbol of American democracy was the New England town meeting, where citizens would gather by the village green to discuss and decide public affairs for their local government. Town meeting self-government should not be overidealized. There were the power elites and the poor in each little town. Yet it did, in an age far simpler than today's, operate on a premise that regular participation in government, beyond merely voting at election time, was an obligation of every citizen. The very format of the town meeting helped assure that that obligation would be fulfilled. The voters *were* the local legislature.

A pundit of 150 years ago might have reasonably predicted that citizen-oriented governmental formats would continue and that citizen efforts would expand as the nation's economic, legal, and technological structures expanded, as growth made people interdependent with one another and with institutions near and far. Such a logical development did not occur; in fact, something closer to the opposite happened. City political machines and city councils replaced the town meetings. Institutions of government and business became bigger and more distant from the people they were supposed to assist or to serve. The power of citizens was delegated to secretive legislatures and executive bureaucracies surrounded and dominated by well-organized special-interest groups that in turn learned that their best investment was the financing or buying of elections. Although increasingly shielded by institutional corruption, complexity, and secrecy from being regularly accountable to the public, government institutions fed the propaganda that elections were enough of a mandate and that such elections were adequately democratic. Especially during the past thirty years, corporations and other special interests have become only bigger and more astute in using governmental power and tax revenues to support their goals and subsidize their treasuries. This interlock between government and business has further complicated the task of citizen effort. For no longer can citizens start with the assumption that government is uncommitted to a special-interest group.

The people's loss of the power to govern themselves has deepened as the need for such self-goverment has risen. Certainly, the costs of citizen powerlessness are accelerating, if only because more people are being affected more ways by more events beyond their control. The American Revolution rang with the declaration that "the price of liberty is eternal vigilance." That is also true for "justice" and "peace" —and for "clean water" and "clean air" and "safe cars" and "healthy work places." But these good things, the blessings of liberty, will not come to pass until we cease viewing citizen involvement as just a privilege and begin defining our daily work to include citizenship toward public problems as an obligation.

This process starts with the individual's use of his or her time and energy. Most people think they are good citizens if they obey the laws and vote at election time. First of all, this is not enough by its own measure because too many people and powerful groups do not obey the laws and almost half the people over eighteen do not vote. But by a broader measure, voting can never be enough simply because decisions affecting people are made by government between elections. It is what citizens do *between* elections that decides whether elections are to be meaningful exercises of debate and decision or whether they are to remain expensive contests between tweedledees and tweedledums. It is not difficult to describe the citizenship gap. How many decisions in Washington, in the state capital, or in the city council involve even modest citizen participation? Why, at all levels of government, does the bureaucracy of executive branch agencies and departments decide matters without the legislature's knowledge or restraint?

The average worker spends about a quarter of his time on the job earning money to pay his taxes but spends virtually no time overseeing the spenders of those taxes. In the marketplace the same disparity between expenditure and involvement prevails. A consumer will spend thousands of hours driving a new automobile or eating food from a supermarket, but can find no way to spend any time to correct the overpricing, fraud, and hazards associated with these products. This is also the case with consumers taking out a loan or purchasing an insurance policy. It is no wonder that in the marketplace or in the halls of government, those who are organized and knowledgeable obtain their way. And those people who abdicate, delegate, or vegetate are taken.

Look at the United States today. Can anyone deny that this country has more problems than it deserves and more solutions than it uses? Its massive wealth, skills, and diversity should never have tolerated, much less endured, the problems and perils that seem to worsen despite a continuing aggregate economic growth. There seems to be less and less relationship between the country's total wealth and its willingness to solve the ills and injustices that beset it. The spirit of pioneering and problem-solving is weak. National, state, and local political leadership is vague at best, manipulative at worst. Facing the world, the United States stands as an uncertain giant with uncertain purposes toward a world in great need of its help and encouragement.

The reversal of these trends requires different leadership, to be sure, but it also requires a new kind of citizenship—public citizenship, part-time-on-the-job, and full-time—that engages in more exercise and less delegation of citizen power. The impulse to become a public citizen can spring from many sources—for example, a fundamental compassion for people and a sense of how inextricably interdependent a society we have. But in a practical, animating way, the spark is learning by doing, developing the techniques and strategies for citizen organization and action. If it can be shown that civic action can solve problems, then more people will shuck their indifference or resignation and want to join the effort.

How much work there is to do can be gauged by how little has been done. Every week, thousands of government agencies are making decisions which will affect the environment, utility rates, food prices and quality, land use, taxes, transportation, health care, employment, job safety, rent, schools, crime, prisons, peace, civil liberties and rights, and many other conditions of social coexistence now and into the future. Surrounding these agencies are lobbyists and advocates for special economic interests, some of whom take jobs for a few years within these agencies to make themselves more useful to their private employers later. Using numerous combinations of the carrot and stick, these pressure groups more often than not get exactly what they want. On rare occasions, a few full-time public interest advocates are present at the scene of the action.

Greatly outnumbered and equipped with only the justice and knowledge of their cause, these full-time citizens have achieved remarkable successes in the courts and before regulatory agencies and legislatures. The national citizens' struggles against the Supersonic Transport (SST), cyclamates, and the laxness of the Atomic Energy Commission neglect of adequate safety standards in nuclear power plants can be paralleled by hundreds of smaller victories at the state and local levels by an aroused citizenry. These Americans have learned that practice makes perfect and the more experience they accumulate, the more effective they become.

Given what a few citizens have done, it is a source of optimism to ask what many, many more like them could do in the future. A look at the past can make future projections of citizen impact more credible. Imagine that twenty-five years ago, citizens concerned about the future quality of life in America—say one out of ten adults—had gotten together to do something about it. Our urban centers would not be choked with cars, or laced with concrete belts that strangle the polluted cities in ever-increasing slums, corruption, crime, noise, and public waste. Our rivers, lakes, and oceans would still be producing untainted fish and would be safe for swimming. Drinking water would not be increasingly imperiled by pollution. The air would not be as filled with vile and violent contaminants, and the land not ravaged by insensitive corporate and government forces wasting our resources faster than they are replenished. Consumers would not be exploited by shoddy goods and services, deceptive practices, and price-fixing that (according to Senator Philip Hart's studies) take at least 25 percent of every consumer dollar.

Thousands of American workers would not be dying or sickened each year because of the toxic chemicals, gases, and dust that pervade so many factories, foundries, and mines. Equal opportunity in education and employment and adequate medical care would have avoided the misery that cruelly affects many Americans. Nor would hunger and poverty have been belatedly "discovered" in the sixties to be affecting some thirty million Americans. Factory and office workers would not be federally taxed 20 percent of their wages while countless men of great wealth are assessed 4 percent or less and many corporations with enormous incomes pay nothing or next to nothing. Small businessmen and homeowners could not be squeezed by powerful corporations whose predatory practices, underpayment of property taxes, and other abuses serve to further concentrate their powers and plunders.

Our Congress and state legislatures would not have continued to be underequipped and indentured to pressure groups instead of monitoring the executive branches and responding to the real needs of all the people. The power and expenditures of the military establishment and their civilian superiors would have been scrutinized, and perhaps curtailed, many painful, costly years ago. Above all, our political system would have reverberated with higher quality and dedication as the momentum of expert citizen movements increased.

A small number of citizens throughout our country's history have kept the flame of citizenship burning brightly to the benefit of millions of their less engaged neighbors. These true patriots have known that democracy comes hard and goes easy. To make democracy work, it takes work—citizen work. Many practical lessons can be learned from their experiences. Today, citizen groups are flowering all over the country, but they need to be better organized, better funded, and staffed with skilled, dedicated, full-time people. New citizen organizations such as Action for Children's Television in Boston (to stop television exploitation of children), Consumer Action Now in New York and Citizen's Action Program in Chicago (getting large industries to stop underpaying their property taxes), and GASP in Pittsburgh (fighting air pollution) are showing what can be done with minimum funds and maximum civic spirit. Courageous public citizens, such as education advocate Julius Hobson in Washington, D.C., are the true unsung heroes of American democracy. They have weathered community pressure to fight for a more just society in cities, towns, and villages around the country.

Many more citizens work to correct small abuses or deficiencies in the community once or twice and then retire to their former state of inaction. Such withdrawal does little to encourage others to engage in similar activities and does nothing to push initial drives beyond symptoms and treadmills to more fundamental reform that lasts. Easy disillusionment, the inability to rebound from difficulties, and lack of stamina must be candidly assessed and overcome through modest amounts of self-discipline. This is done in athletics and games all the time; it should also become the practice in the citizenship arena.

This *Public Citizen's Action Manual* is designed to help the growth of lasting, imaginative, effective citizen action. It is *not* premised on the notion that only people with leisure time who are fairly well off can use the advice suggested in the following pages. Instead, the projects and guidelines described in this book are predicated on the belief that citizen effort is everybody's business and that everybody can engage in such effort. Who, for example, is better equipped to fight for women's rights or conduct consumer surveys than women, all too many of whom may be wasting much of their time daily watching soap operas, gossiping on the telephone, or "keeping in their place"? Who is better situated to further the job safety laws than workers exposed to occupational hazards and capable of organizing themselves or invigorating their unions to humanize the workplace? Who could be better motivated to reform the motor clubs than the disenfranchised members of these clubs—the millions of motorists? Who should be more inclined to expose the gross underpayment of property taxes by large companies than homeowners, small businessmen, and taxpayers generally? These are not wholly rhetorical questions. There are people who have indeed done all these things with some success. Had they been joined by some of the 99.999 percent of their neighbors, co-workers, or co-members who were inactive, truly enduring progress would have taken place. Sometimes one or two individuals are enough; over two million Chevrolets were recalled for defects because of one inspector in a GM plant speaking out; cyclamates were taken off the market because of two outspoken scientists in the Food and Drug Administration. For the most part, however, there is need for organization around public issues particularly when the hurdles are high and the facts are not yet available to the public.

The projects outlined in this book, as Donald Ross points out, are not all-inclusive. They represent just a sample of the kinds of problems that affect many people and that can be worked on by many people. They help show the way to overcome the early inhibitions against getting started on an unknown terrain. Citizenship is not an endeavor reserved only for the most talented; anybody can do it and everybody should do it. This manual offers readers interested in consumer protection, health issues, equal opportunity, taxes, government bureaucracy, and citizen organizing an abundance of factual and advisory materials. It is a book to use and to surpass. The faster this book becomes obsolete for the user, the faster his or her citizen know-how will advance. For once you tackle one or more of the problems in your community that are herein described, you will come up with new sources of information, new strategies, new allies, new understanding of how the objects of your reform effort will respond. I hope you will send us summaries of your experiences and any further ideas which will strengthen the sections in this book or add new problems to be presented for citizen resolution.

The exercise by citizens of their rights and responsibilities is what makes a working democracy ever sensitive to the just needs of its people. Such citizen effort is a learning process which can be increasingly advanced with practice. For increasing numbers of Americans, citizenship should become a full-time career role, supported by other citizens, to work on major institutions of government and business for a better society. It is this fundamental role of the *public citizen* in a democracy that must attract more adherents and supporters from across America.

Ralph Nader
Washington, D.C.

Author's Note

The purpose of this book is to begin to answer two questions repeated time and again by people concerned about their country: "What can I do to improve it?" and "How can I do it?" There are no final answers to these questions. What we have tried to do in this manual is gather together projects which can serve as models for constructive action.

Measured against the sum of society's ills, individual projects may seem small, almost insignificant. A Buyer's Action Center, for example, can't tame the multi-national corporation. Nor can a Legislator's Scorecard by itself make congressmen responsive to the people who elect them. But it is our conviction that such small projects are the building blocks of a larger citizen movement. Small successes are preferable to large defeats and an achievement in one area opens up possibilities in others. Furthermore, as citizens realize that they *can* make a difference, more projects will be launched.

Thus the projects contained in this book can become the tools of change. The responsibility for using them rests with each reader.

Contents

I

PROJECTS
TO PROTECT
THE CONSUMER

Anyone who buys anything at any time is a consumer. At one time or another, most consumers buy short-weighted meat, defective appliances, spoiled food, poorly constructed furniture, or bad service. They may be the victims of fraudulent credit schemes, deceptive advertisements, or cleverly worded warranties which take away their rights. For some, consumer fraud is perennial and especially serious; the poor, the undereducated, those with language difficulties, migrant workers, the very young, and the very old are the hardest hit. They are also the ones least able to bear the loss.

Because consumer abuse affects everyone, it is an excellent issue around which to rally support and build a community organization. Most consumers realize that as individuals confronting major national manufacturers or retailers, they can seldom hope to emerge victorious in disputes over shoddy goods or fraudulent services. There is a clear and urgent need to organize, to pool resources, to combine

efforts so that individually and collectively consumers will
be better protected.

Each project in this section is designed to further the
cause of consumer protection. Some of the projects can be
undertaken by individual consumers acting alone; others
require group effort. Some can be carried out quickly and
easily; others, such as the projects to create a Buyers Action Center and Automobile Safety and Complaint Center,
are institution-building efforts requiring considerable time
and money. Some bring an instant response; the effect of
others is felt only cumulatively. In all cases, however, a
project should not be viewed as an end in itself but as a
model or steppingstone for other projects, each promoting
the cause of consumer protection.

How to Detect and Correct Fraudulent Repair Practices

When a person goes to have a pair of shoes repaired, a
tennis racquet restrung, a suit mended, or a scratch on a
fender repainted, there is seldom any question about the
nature of the problem or its solution. The repairer may
try to sell the person a new item instead of repairing the
old one or he may do shoddy work, but in either case, the
consumer has a way of evaluating his need and the quality
of the work performed. If the body shop, for example, suggests a complete paint job instead of touching up the
scratched fender, the consumer can understand the alter-
natives and evaluate the pros and cons of each. But when
a stereo set develops an unnecessary buzz or warble, a television picture turns hazy or goes blank, or a car stalls at
every red light, most consumers haven't the faintest idea
what caused the problem or what is required to fix it.

Stereos, televisions, and cars employ relatively complex modern technology. Consequently, the owner is at the mercy of the specialist who knows or is supposed to know whether the TV needs a new picture tube costing sixty dollars or only a sixty-cent fuse.

In most states the repair industry controls and regulates itself. The results of this policy are that the repair "racket," as it is bitterly known by disgruntled consumers, has bilked the unwary of billions of dollars a year in unnecessary work. In some industries, the incidence of fraudulent or sloppy repair work has reached epidemic proportions. Senator Philip Hart's Senate Subcommittee on Antitrust and Monopoly summarized the findings of a two-year study of automobile repair practices:

American consumers spend 25 to 30 billion dollars a year on auto repair. Various studies on the quality of the work were presented to us. They rated the poor, unneeded, or not done work at amounts ranging from 36 percent to 99 percent. Even taking the low figure, that means consumers are wasting 8 to 10 billion dollars that they lay out for auto repair yearly.

Government and citizen probes into television repair have revealed similar abuses.

Consumer discontent has forced some local and state government agencies to begin licensing and regulating repairers, but this movement is still embryonic. Pressure from citizen activists can help speed up the process of reform and ensure that the licensing statute provides strong enforcement provisions; unannounced inspections, stiff fines, and mandatory training provisions are essential if the law is to have any teeth.

A citizens group can help build support for the licensing of repairers by conducting an investigation of local repair practices. The most effective way to study repair practices is to attempt to get an item fixed. The technique used is to take a vehicle, appliance, or other consumer item in good repair, make a small adjustment that disables it or makes it function poorly, and then take it in for repair.

The analysis of what is wrong and the estimate of repair
cost will indicate how competent and trustworthy the repairer is. The projects described below are models that
can be duplicated using other products.

SOME WAYS TO EVALUATE AUTOMOBILE
REPAIR SHOPS

Poorly trained or unscrupulous mechanics are infamous
for "sunshine" repair jobs: the owner brings the car
in for repair and the mechanic parks it in the lot for a
week and returns it with a hefty bill for labor. They are
also known for their ability to turn a minor malfunction
into a complete overhaul or the replacement of major systems, such as the carburetor, battery, starter, ignition system, and so on. To determine whether a fraud is being
perpetrated, a car in good condition can first be "gimmicked" and then taken in for a repair estimate.

Cars in good repair can be gimmicked in the following
ways:

1. The "dead" battery. Remove one of the battery cables.
Wipe an insulating material on the battery post (best is
some of the white or blue substance found around the
battery post of an older car). Replace the cable, but do
not tighten it too much. Check your work by trying to
start the car—the engine should not turn over. If the
mechanic does not check for this condition first, but tries to
sell you a new battery or starter, he fails the test.

2. Ignition problems. Badly adjusted ignition points usually will not disable a vehicle, but they will make it run
very poorly. Remove the distributor cap and make the
ignition point gap either too narrow or too wide (so that
they just barely open on the high side of the cam or barely
close on the low side). This will not only cause the point
gap to be off, but will throw the ignition timing off. After

adjusting, do not tighten the hold-down screw any more than barely necessary to hold the points in place. If the mechanic tries to sell a tune-up, say that you had the car tuned a few months ago, and that it just recently began to run badly. If he won't do a quick check of the ignition adjustments, or if he cannot make the car run right in a couple of minutes, he flunks.

3. Carburetor. By turning one or both of the idle mixture screws nearly closed or several turns too far open, you can make the vehicle run very poorly or stall at idle. The mechanic should be able to diagnose and fix this in about one minute flat. If he wants to overhaul or to replace the carburetor, or do a tune-up, he flunks.

4. Defective parts. Obtain a defective part—an ignition capacitor, starter solonoid, regulator, or what-not. Install it in place of a part in good condition. This tests the mechanic's diagnostic ability, although he may take more than a few minutes to find the problem. Beware the mechanic who merely begins replacing parts without making sure the part being replaced is bad.

Some final points: it is best to have your own mechanic disable your vehicle, so he can fix it again if the mechanic you are testing cannot. Also, when the vehicle is un-fixed, don't leave telltale signs that it has been tampered with—you may have a very angry mechanic on your hands if he suspects that you have been testing him. Finally, be prepared to pay all charges. Some shops have a minimum charge of five dollars or more; whether the mechanic has passed or failed your test, he will expect payment for his time.

TELEVISION REPAIR

During March and April of 1972 three law students from the American University Law School undertook an investigation of television repair practices in Montgomery County,

Maryland.* They first checked the files of the County Consumer Protection Agency to locate stores against which complaints had frequently been lodged. Next they contacted a technician in the county school system who agreed to "fix" a TV set so that an average person would think that something was wrong with the picture tube. To accomplish this, a fuse was removed from the high-voltage section of a set in perfect working condition. Without the fuse no electricity could reach the picture tube and the screen went blank. A repairman, depending on his competence and honesty, could replace the fuse or try to sell a new picture tube.

This done, they took the set to a series of repair shops to get repair estimates. An account of one such visit is described below:

The next repair shop the set was taken to was the Potomac Valley Electronics, 7301 MacArthur Blvd., Glen Echo, Md. The files of both the Montgomery County Office of Consumer Affairs and the Maryland State Consumer Protection Division had complaints regarding Potomac Valley Electronics.

The television was taken in March 27, 1972, and we were told the estimate would be available the next day. Upon returning the next day, we were told the picture tube was bad and that the cost of replacing it would be $40.00. The man said he realized this was expensive and asked if we would be interested in buying a new or used television instead of having our set repaired. We, of course, said no, paid the $6.00 estimate fee and left.

After this visit, the technician who was working with the student investigators stated that it appeared that the high-voltage section of the set had never been touched. In other words, the students concluded, "Potomac Valley Electronics had made their estimate solely on the lack of a picture."

* Peter Lynch, Marc Reader, and David Richin are the three students; this project is based on their work.

REMEDIES

If a survey uncovers evidence of fraud by many shops, it should be released at a special press conference, specifying which repair shops were surveyed, how many times each shop was visited, and some details about the estimates of repairs. Although exposure of consumer cheats may serve as a warning, it is unlikely to curb the abuse for long. For the unscrupulous, the risk of exposure is quickly outweighed by the excessive profits that fraudulent repairs generate. Therefore, to avoid creating a one-day splash of publicity with no follow-up, pressure should continue to be applied after the survey is released.

One way to do this is to contact legislators at an early stage of the investigation and get them to agree to hold hearings after the results are released. The student investigators from American University took an additional step and drafted a statute to license television and electronic repair dealers. This legislation is pending before the County Council of Montgomery County.*

Even if the appropriate legislative body refuses to consider a licensing provision, there is much that citizen activists can do to force change. One excellent tactic is to hold well-publicized citizen hearings at which complainants to various consumer departments, merchants, members of the Better Business Bureau, and other interested people would be invited to testify. (See page 179 for suggestions on how to hold citizen hearings.) Pressure can be applied as well to the local consumer agency to prod it into action.

More aggressive citizen groups can engage in consumer picketing and distribute leaflets naming the stores that

* Professor Robert Vaughn, American University Law School, Washington, D.C., will send a copy of this statute to interested citizen groups. Senator Vance Hartke, U.S. Senate, Washington, D.C., has materials available regarding licensing and certification procedures for automobile mechanics.

chronically cheat consumers. Follow-up studies can focus on the worst offenders in an attempt to show that a one-time effort won't work and to drive officials into taking action. Finally, pressure can be brought to bear on those who facilitate the fraud. Better Business Bureaus, Merchants Associations, and Chambers of Commerce that stand by and do nothing should be openly criticized. So should those who indirectly profit from the fraud. Consumer cheats often take out large ads in the Yellow Pages or on radio and television promising "special repair service," "long warranties," or "free estimates." Without advertising, these lures would be ineffective; responsible public utilities and those licensed to use the public airwaves, it can be argued, should not aid inveterate cheats.

How to Protect Shoppers

Consumers have to work hard to shop wisely. It is their task to sort out competing claims and to pressure businesses into providing the highest quality commodities at the lowest possible prices. They apply this pressure each time they choose one brand over another or one retailer over another. One important factor underlying this choice is price differences among competing brands or competing stores. Consideration of quality, convenience, cleanliness, and service are also important, of course. But for many consumers, especially the poor, price is the deciding factor.

The two projects described in this section enable consumers to evaluate price differences. Unit pricing allows comparison among competing brands within a store. Retail price comparisons give information on price differences among competing stores. These projects can be undertaken separately or jointly as part of a major consumer rights movement.

UNIT PRICING

A visit to the cold cereal counter in any supermarket should convince the skeptical of the need for unit pricing. What the shopper will see are three or four tiers of brightly colored boxes of varying sizes and shapes, stretching for five to ten yards down an aisle. Assuming that price alone is the major factor in deciding which cereal to buy, how would the shopper figure out which box offers the most cereal at the cheapest price? The canny consumer, of course, would quickly eliminate the sugar- or chocolate-covered nutritional-nothings promoted for children. Without exception these are overpriced. Even with this deletion, there still remains a bewildering number of choices in odd-sized boxes—1½, 11, 17, or 23 ounces—at different prices—$0.15, $0.59, $0.61 or 2 for $0.91—making a choice based on price alone almost impossible for the average consumer. Selecting the "giant economy size" is no guarantee of real economy; often it is more expensive per ounce than intermediate or regular sizes.

Unit pricing, as its name implies, ignores box shapes and sizes and reduces price information to a uniform standard, such as price per ounce, or price per pound, or price per quart. Using the unit pricing system currently enforced in New York City for cereal, the least expensive brand, in the cheapest-sized box, can be discovered in less than a minute. Next to the cereal counter, merchants are required to display a computer print-out listing the per unit cost of each box of cereal. A glance down the price per ounce column instantly reveals the lowest priced cereal. Other cities which enforce unit pricing use different systems. In Washington, D.C., the actual price and the unit price of each brand are displayed on a label attached to the shelf below each brand. Some manufacturers now print the unit cost directly onto the label. Whichever system is used, even one applied only to selected items, the shopper obtains a useful shopping tool.

Consumers should not expect the food industry to institute unit pricing on its own or even to welcome it when it is proposed by consumers. Since unit pricing cuts through much of the appeal of advertising lures or shelf placement, the industry naturally feels threatened by it. If consumers want unit pricing, they must pressure for its adoption and be ready to overcome industry opposition. A campaign to institute unit pricing must begin by learning how the system operates. The best way to do this is to visit a store employing the system and observe it in operation.

It is worth making an attempt to convince store managers in a community to adopt unit pricing voluntarily. Generally their response will be verbally sympathetic, but they will offer an array of excuses—expense, difficulty, inconvenience—to justify their refusal to implement such a system. All these excuses are belied by the experience of the stores who already use this system. It is important to take this step, however, because it can save energy and time if successful, and also avoid later claims that stores would have instituted unit pricing voluntarily if only someone had asked.

More than likely, it will be necessary to marshal consumer support for unit pricing. Local consumer groups, chapters of women's clubs, unions, and many other organizations not often considered activist can usually be won over to support this program if they are shown how inadequate the present pricing system is and how unit pricing will improve it. Dramatic presentations can be effective. The Minnesota Public Interest Research Group (MPIRG), in its campaign for unit pricing, carried two heads of identically priced lettuce, one weighing 14½ ounces and one weighing 25½ ounces, into a Minneapolis city council meeting to demonstrate how consumers were being gypped because lettuce was priced by the head instead of by the ounce. Loaves of bread, bags of fruit, cans of olives, boxes of cold cereals, and numerous other commodities can provide similar flagrant examples of consumer abuse.

Another method for gaining consumer support is to prepare a model unit pricing survey and hand it out to shoppers as they enter the store. Twenty or twenty-five popular items should be arranged on the list in easy to read columns. An accompanying leaflet can explain the purpose of unit pricing and what the shopper can do to help get the system adopted.

One way to demonstrate support is to collect signatures on petitions. Petitions can be circulated in front of churches, at social gatherings, or from tables set up in front of local supermarkets. Sometimes, if widespread support is demonstrated, local merchants will agree to institute unit pricing voluntarily. They may try to exact concessions over how many items it will cover or how it will be applied; organizers of the campaign must be vigilant and tough and not be tricked into a weak compromise. Remember, if the food industry in a community suggests a compromise, it means they are feeling the pressure. The initiative must not be lost and the campaign should be pressed to get the best possible unit pricing system.

If unit pricing is not adopted voluntarily, there should be an attempt to impose it by law. First, you should collect samples of legislation enacted in other cities to show that the proposal is not a radical departure from established practices. A model proposal combining the best provisions of these laws should be drawn up. You should also attempt to line up bipartisan support within the council to introduce appropriate legislation. A dramatic way to present the proposal is to appear before the council meeting armed with endorsements from local community groups and examples of deceptively packaged food items. MPIRG attracted publicity by distributing a consumer "quiz" to members of the Minneapolis council.* The quiz contained such questions as the following:

Q. Heinz ketchup is sold in two sizes. Which is the better buy: the large "ketchup lover's" size, 26 ounces for $0.55; or the regular size, which is 14 ounces for $0.29?

A. The regular is a better buy at $0.0207 per ounce.

Since the press should be notified of the presentation, the displays must be visually attractive, particularly if television cameras are likely to be present. Large charts showing comparative prices can be especially effective.

After the initial flurry of publicity attending the presentation, continued pressure should be applied by letters to newspapers, speeches to community meetings, and attempts to get additional endorsements (including editorial support). If the issue is allowed to fade away, it may be tabled or ignored by legislators not anxious to offend large business interests in the community. Therefore, sustained consumer activity must keep the issue hot.

RETAIL PRICE COMPARISONS

Unit pricing enables consumers to select the lowest priced brand names once inside the store. A retail price comparison, on the other hand, enables consumers to compare prices among stores. It is almost impossible for a consumer, acting alone, to compare shopping values among different stores. But with price information pooled, it immediately becomes apparent which merchants charge the lowest and which the highest prices. Price differences can be considerable. One Washington, D.C., survey found price disparities averaging 13 percent between supermarkets. On a few items, the disparities rose as high as 40 percent.

A system of shared information can be developed simply

* A copy of the MPIRG materials and press clippings can be obtained by writing Ms. Sue Klein, MPIRG, 3036 University Avenue, S. E., Minneapolis, Minnesota 55414.

by organizing the efforts consumers already expend on their individual shopping trips. By collecting price data, tabulating it, and then publishing the comparison in a suitable form, a handful of citizens can have a significant effect on prices and merchandising practices within their own communities. In Hawaii, where the first consumer-sponsored price comparisons were undertaken, *supermarket prices dropped an average of 4 percent* in the four months following the introduction of the comparisons. In Washington, D.C., shortly after the results of price surveys received wide publicity, Grand Union food stores, the highest priced chain in the survey, began to cut prices.

Retail price comparisons can also show:

1. Price differences between chains. These are often dramatic, as the Washington, D.C., survey mentioned above showed.

2. Price differences among stores in the same chain. These, contrary to popular belief, are common. A Washington, D.C., survey of Peoples Drug Stores, the capital's largest chain, found a difference of 12 percent between the highest and lowest priced stores in the chain, with, again, enormous gaps for some items.

3. Price differences among different areas of the city. A Columbus, Ohio, price comparison showed student communities near Ohio State University and residents of ghetto areas paying significantly more than suburban shoppers.

4. Price differences among product categories, such as meats, produce, dairy and canned goods. Stores ranked closely overall may have wide price disparities among different product categories.

After a few comparisons, the patterns will become apparent. Surveyors can even check to see whether a sale is used to disguise subsequent price increases (lowering the price of an item for a sale and then raising it again higher than it was before), whether prices jump in ghetto areas or areas where many elderly people live when welfare and social security checks arrive, and whether price stabilization programs are effective.

Consumer-sponsored retail price comparisons have been tested in Hartford, Connecticut; Columbus, Ohio; Chicago, Illinois; Minneapolis, Minnesota; and Washington, D.C. Based on their experiences, a complete how-to-do-it kit has been developed and is available to interested groups. Two ingredients are needed to conduct, tabulate, and disseminate the survey. The first is a task force of volunteers to do the research, and the second is a few minutes' access to a computer. (Small surveys can be tabulated by hand, but a computer is the only practical way to conduct large supermarket surveys.) Survey results can be disseminated through the news media or in leaflets distributed by members of the survey team.

Step 1: Preparing the Survey List

It is impossible to survey every item in a store since the average supermarket stocks over seven thousand items. However, a representative sampling of a small number of items can serve as a basis for a valid comparison among stores. The list should reflect the relative importance of items in a typical consumer's market basket. The following "market basket breakdown" is based on surveys conducted by the A&P supermarket chain* and the Bureau of Labor Statistics (BLS).†

The problem of quality comparability between stores can be solved by surveying only national name brands— checking the price of Campbell's pork and beans in three different stores, for example. When there is no name brand, as with fresh meats and poultry, the same grade or cut should be surveyed. For example, all fresh beef products surveyed should be U.S. Choice. If chicken is surveyed, whole chickens, breasts, backs, or wings should be specified. Produce causes more problems. Some stores

* "How Different Consumers Shop the Modern Supermarket," Part 7 of the A&P Study, *Progressive Grocer*, October 1970.
† *"Relative Importance of Components in the Consumer Price Index*, 1970."

MARKET BASKET BREAKDOWN

Type of Purchase	Percentage of Consumer Expenditures in Supermarkets
Meats, poultry, fish (Within this category, beef and veal account for 40% of consumer expenditures; pork for 23%; other meats, including processed meats such as hot dogs and salami, for 17%; poultry for 11%; and fish for 9%)	28
Produce (Within this category, fresh vegetables account for 58% of consumer expenditures; fresh fruits for 42%)	7
Dairy (including eggs and ice cream)	10
Bakery and cereals (including packaged cookies and crackers)	7
Frozen foods (including frozen juice concentrates)	3
Processed fruits and vegetables (Within this category, canned vegetables account for 40% of consumer expenditures; canned fruits for 26%; juices and drinks for 26%; and dried vegetables and fruits for 8%)	5
Staples (including flour, sugar, coffee, tea, shortenings and oils, baking supplies, and pasta)	5
Miscellaneous prepared foods (ketchup, soup, mayonnaise, peanut butter, etc.)	20
Nonfoods (including laundry supplies, cleaning aids, paper products, cigarettes, and health and beauty aids)	15

sell oranges by the bag, others by the dozen or by the pound. The survey requires standardization—items sold in different ways should be dropped from the survey list.

Generally, only the most popular items should be surveyed. If sales data indicating the most popular brands are unavailable, allocation of shelf space within stores provides a rough estimate. The more popular the item, the more shelf space it will get. Store brands present a special problem since many of the large chains sell their own brands in addition to standard brands. Prices of store brands usually average about 15 to 20 percent below those of name brands. In a community with several major supermarket chains, one section of the survey might be devoted to a comparison among various store brands.

The number of items on a list should be large enough to provide a good cross-section of the market, but not so large as to overburden surveyors. A 100-item list is a good size though smaller lists are adequate for drug stores, convenience stores, or appliance stores.

Step 2: Organizing a Volunteer Surveying Force

The idea of comparing prices sells itself. It is a project that most people would like to see done but can't do on their own. Finding volunteer surveyors, therefore, is usually not a problem. Notices to community groups should attract enough volunteers. In addition, citizen groups like the League of Women Voters may want to cosponsor the project and eventually take over the project themselves.

The size of the volunteer force depends on the geographical limits of the survey and the number of items to be surveyed. For maximum impact, prices within a single neighborhood or area of the city should be compared. In the suburbs, town-by-town surveys probably are best. However, it is sometimes useful to compare prices in different counties, towns, or neighborhoods to gauge regional differences.

The amount of time required of each surveyor varies

depending on the number of items to be checked, the number of stores, and the surveyor's familiarity with the assigned stores. A 100-item grocery survey usually takes about an hour to accomplish, and about five minutes to report the results by phone. The survey can be done at the shopper's convenience, so long as it is completed within a two- or three-day period.

Step 3: Conducting the Survey

Before the survey list is distributed to volunteers, a preliminary check should be run on the availability of items. If a few stores have all of the items to be surveyed, it is safe to go ahead. At this time it is necessary to call a meeting of volunteer surveyors. The meeting should be repeated two or three times on different days and at different times to ensure that all surveyors can be present.

At each meeting, the names, addresses, and phone numbers of volunteers should be collected, and in turn the volunteers should be given a phone number where they can receive assistance from a survey organizer if they encounter problems. The procedures of the survey should be explained carefully and each surveyor should receive a packet containing an identification card or letter of introduction (to avoid problems with store managers), an instruction sheet, and a survey list. The survey list should provide space for the store name, address, and the date of the survey.

Step 4: Analyzing the Data

The brunt of the data analysis is most easily handled by the computer. The citizens group may be able to obtain free computer time from a local college or high school. But if the computer time has to be bought from a commercial source, the cost for each survey should be less than twenty dollars per run. The telephone Yellow Pages of most medium-sized cities list data processing companies that can perform this service. The first survey will be the hardest, since the procedures of data analysis will be new and every price for every store will have to be key punched—fed into the computer. Many high schools and most colleges teach key punching, so an operator should be easy to find. Subsequent surveys will be easier since only price changes will have to be recorded.

The results from the computer will only be as good as the information put in. *Accuracy is critical.* An "eyeball" comparison of data can help to eliminate gross errors by catching items wildly out of line with other stores and re-checking the data. Often, however, the error is not the surveyor's but the store's. One Washington, D.C., survey revealed mispricing on about 2 percent of supermarket items surveyed.

After the preliminary check, the data can be fed into the computer. The person in charge of programming the computer can teach volunteers to key punch. Once the technique is mastered, a 100-item survey should take about twenty minutes to key punch.

Step 5: Releasing the Results

The results of the first survey should be released at a major press conference. If surveys are conducted regularly, results should be distributed to the press by means of subsequent survey press releases. Some groups contract with newspapers to provide the papers with survey results on a regular basis in exchange for a small fee to cover phone, printing, and computer costs.

Not all results should be released in the first survey. If 100 items are surveyed, only 40 or 50 should be identified to prevent stores from selectively reducing prices to look good the next time around. (For the same reason store managers should *never* be shown the list.) Different mixes of 50 items should be released in each new survey. If a survey is repeated more than a dozen times, new items should be substituted on the survey list.

If the local paper, which depends on supermarkets for advertising revenue, refuses to print the results, other newspapers and radio and television should be contacted concerning this denial of media access. In addition, the results can be disseminated through leaflets distributed in front of supermarkets and posted in churches or community halls. The highlights can be broadcast over radio and television.

Retail price comparisons are an easy way to bring citizen groups together to demonstrate the impact of organized citizen action. But the goal of the organizing group should not be to continue the surveys indefinitely. Eventually a local government agency should take over the survey as one of its official functions. Alternatively, a town or city council could require stores to submit their price lists to a government agency, which would compare the prices and release the information to consumers.

INSTRUCTIONS FOR COMPILING DATA FOR THE VERMONT PUBLIC INTEREST RESEARCH GROUP FOOD PRICE SURVEY

Purpose: To inform consumers which stores consistently charge less for identical or similar items, so that each consumer may save money; and to stimulate competition between stores which could lead to lower prices citywide.

Teams: Two people per team per store.

Time: Plan to spend forty-five minutes to an hour and a half in each store, depending on your experience with the survey itself and the store's layout.

Methods: Either of the following methods work well; their efficiency depends on your preference:
   a. Partners may price items together at same time, or
   b. Partners may separate and survey every item individually and compare results *before leaving store;* please correct discrepancies.

You will discover several ways to decrease your time and energies as you become experienced. *As long as your recorded prices are absolutely correct, use whatever methods best suit you and your partner.*

If you cannot find an item: Ask any clerk for its location.

If you cannot find the size or particular brand: Ask clerk (or manager) what the usual price is.

A word about conscientiousness: If you do not record a price for an item, the item must be scrapped from every list in the final tabulation. This practice wastes other teams' time and energies, and lessens the scope of the survey. PLEASE BE THOROUGH.

If the sales person explains that the store does not carry a particular item: Place an X in the item's price space.

Specials, sales, etc.: Place an asterisk (*) beside the item's price.

Attitudes: Some personnel will be exceedingly cooperative and offer their help by showing you where everything is and telling you their prices.

Some personnel will be exceedingly apprehensive and try to make you feel uncomfortable.

Smile and thank both types. Try to put them at ease by being firm in your conviction of the values of such a survey.

Some shoppers will ask you what you are doing: Show them the results in the most recent newsletter and let them keep a copy.

You might be approached by someone pointing out faults with the survey. Explain that we are open to their suggestions, and write them down for VPIRG review.

How to Ferret Out and Help Eliminate "Bait and Switch" Advertising

"Bait and switch" advertising is a means by which unscrupulous merchants lure customers into a store by offering a bargain and then use unfair practices to persuade them to buy a different product. The Federal Trade Commission defines this practice in the following way:

an alluring but insincere offer to sell a product or service which the advertiser in truth does not want or intend to sell. Its purpose is to switch customers from buying the advertised product in order to sell something else usually at a higher price or on a basis more advantageous to the advertiser. The primary aim is to obtain leads as to persons interested in buying merchandise of the type so advertised.

Both the Federal Trade Commission and many states outlaw these practices. The statute in Oregon is typical:

[It is illegal to] advertise goods and services with intent not to sell them as advertised or with the intent not to supply reasonably expectable public demand unless the advertisement discloses a limitation of quantity. (ORS 646.608)

Bait and switch advertising plays on the weakness of the consumer and depends for its success on the skills of high-pressure sales people. Obviously a consumer answering an ad for a new $1,895 automobile can simply say no when the salesman takes him by the arm and leads him over to the $2,249 cars. But a fast-talking salesman can bamboozle a surprising number of people who will not realize what is happening.

During the summer of 1972, the Oregon Student Public Interest Research Group (OSPIRG) studied bait and switch advertising in the Portland area. They investigated automobile dealerships, a Sears Roebuck store, a sewing machine store, and a store selling outdoor equipment. One or more volunteers posing as buyers would enter the store with a copy of an advertisement and ask to see the item advertised. The reaction of sales people and the availability and condition of the advertised merchandise determined whether bait and switch was being practiced. Some examples from investigators reports indicate the most common tactics of bait and switch.

The general pattern at the outdoor store was for salesmen to show the customer to the sleeping bags on sale which were wrapped up tightly in plastic and then, after casually stating that the sale bag could not be unwrapped because "the down falls out," switch them to a more expensive bag conveniently displayed at full length. The OSPIRG investigator visited Sears eight times during a four-day sale on black-and-white television sets. On seven out of the eight visits, he was told that Sears was sold out, a clear violation of the Oregon statute quoted above. An even more striking example of bait and switch tactics was recorded at a Ford dealership. The following is an excerpt from the OSPIRG Report:

My wife and I walked into the showroom at about 4:20 P.M. We were both dressed informally, but I felt that we looked likely prospects for the LTD (right age, man, and wife, etc.). We walked in the front door and were met by a man who later identified himself as J. B. Johnson. I walked up to him and with the piece of paper in my hand asked him if they had that $2,991 LTD that I had read about in the paper. He said, "Oh, that ad just came out today. That's a stripped-down car—you wouldn't be interested. I'm not sure that we've got any in. All of those ad cars are order cars" (meaning that they have to be ordered specially). I persisted and informed him again that I was interested in the car. He said that he had only worked there for a few days and did not know if they had it around or not. He again disparaged the car by saying that it was a stripped-down car, had a standard transmission, no heater, no air conditioning and that I probably wouldn't like it. He continued to talk down the car as he walked around the showroom. As he walked around the showroom, he pointed out a Ford LTD Brougham for a price of about $5,600. I protested and informed him again that I was interested in the $2,991 LTD. Again he disparaged the product, and said that we should see more cars. He took us up three floors in the elevator and took us into a back showroom. He then proceeded to show us a Gran Torino, a Thunderbird, and several more LTD's, all costing $4,500 and up. He made us an offer on a 1972 LTD hardtop 2-door that listed at about $4,300. He said that he would knock off $350 of that price, making it $3,950. As we were riding up in the elevator, my wife asked Mr. Johnson if we were going to be able to see the LTD for $2,991. Again he disparaged the product, and added that he would have to order the car, and that it would take at least 60 days to get it.

In Oregon, county district attorneys and the state attorney general's office used the OSPIRG data to force the worst violators to sign orders stating that they would not engage in similar practices in the future. OSPIRG is now investigating other stores and will monitor those who signed compliance orders to ensure that they hold to their agreements.

Citizen activists can duplicate OSPIRG's investigation anywhere they suspect merchants are using bait and switch tactics. All that is needed are would-be purchasers who look and can act the part, an understanding of how bait and switch works and the perseverance to check and recheck each suspected store.

Some common types of bait and switch tactics are the following:

1. Accepting a deposit for an advertised product, then switching to a higher-priced item;

2. Failure to make delivery of the advertised product within a reasonable time, or failure to make a refund;

3. Disparagement by act or words of the advertised product, or disparagement of the guarantee, credit terms, availability of service, or repairs. This may be the most common tactic.

4. Failure to have an advertised product in stock.

In connection with automobile advertising, bait and switch may consist of the following:

1. Placing the car in an inaccessible place—the back of the lot, a garage annex, or in some other way making it difficult for the purchaser to locate the vehicle.

2. Advertising a car that disparages itself by its condition, lack of options, or color. In one OSPIRG investigation, a newspaper ad showed a Pinto with bumper guards, side chrome, chrome strips underneath doors, white sidewalls, and wheel covers. The car the investigators were shown when they came to the lot had none of these options and was "an ugly brown beige color."

3. Salesmen appearing to know little about the advertised car, i.e., location in the lot, price, performance statistics, equipment.

Once data is collected, it can be published in report form naming the offending merchants and describing precisely the tactics used. The report should also be turned over to the local consumer agency, the city council, and the district attorney. If a local or state statute exists, a demand should be made for the proper authorities to take action. Or the city council or state legislature should be urged to pass a law, if none is on the books.

More information regarding the mechanics of bait and switch can be obtained from OSPIRG, 411 Governor Building, 408 S.W. Second Avenue, Portland, Oregon 97204.

How to Reform the Automobile Association of America

The Automobile Association of America (AAA) is the largest association of automobile owners in the United States. It is made up of 230 affiliated automobile clubs which have a combined membership of over 15 million individuals. AAA members constitute the largest organized body of consumers of automobile products and services. Because it is an association of *owners*, rather than manufacturers, dealers, or repairers, the member clubs of the AAA should be vigilant protectors of the driver's welfare. Sadly, they are not.

The main activities of AAA clubs are providing road service if a member's car breaks down, selling insurance, providing "triptiks" (easy-to-read road maps), certifying motels and hotels, making travel arrangements (AAA is the largest travel agency in the United States), and selling their own "club" brand tires, batteries and other automobile equipment. AAA clubs also publish magazines, lobby before state legislatures and Congress, and sponsor driver safety programs.

Because of the number of drivers it represents, the AAA should be the leading advocate of safe car construction and other reforms, such as increased funding for mass transit, which would untangle traffic and benefit drivers. Instead, it has become an ally of the automobile industry and highway lobby. AAA is opposed to higher safety standards on grounds of expense to the consumer, while not protesting the even greater cost of styling superficialities. It has, at the same time, ignored the high cost of deaths, injuries, and high insurance premiums due to unsafe cars. Clearly, the AAA could use its considerable muscle to pressure for better warranty provisions for new cars; it does not. It could certify automobile repair shops or provide diagnostic services for its members; only two clubs, Missouri and San Francisco, maintain their own diagnostic centers and one licenses diagnostics centers. None certify repairers. In short, the AAA and its member clubs have almost completely abdicated their responsibilities in automotive safety and have neglected the consumer.

Rating hotels, for example, used to be important. But now the great motel and hotel chains with their brand names in effect provide their own identification. What is the difference between a New York Holiday Inn and one in Omaha, Miami, or San Diego? Of course, the AAA rating does help independent motel operators. But the overwhelming majority of AAA members would be better served by ratings of repair shops and garages. Even the AAA road service, which for many people provides the sole reason for joining the association, is now offered more cheaply by other organizations.

The AAA has stagnated for several reasons, but principally because management is out of touch with the membership. In many clubs control is a "family affair" exercised by close business associates; in most clubs elections are simply not held or are rigged in favor of the present management in a variety of ways. In both the Georgia Auto Club and the Minnesota State Auto Association, for example, directors of AAA clubs are picked by the directors themselves. Regular members have no vote. In Chicago, the AAA club is reported to have two classes of members —the 300,000 who can't vote and the 12 who can. In Indiana, the directors of the Hoosier Motor Club are picked by the "active members"—but an "annual member" only becomes an active member when the board of directors makes him one. More often, members have a theoretical voting right, but management maintains control by getting proxies from all new members, and by spending thousands of dollars of club money (as much as $100,000 a year in one case) to keep management proxies under their control. This procedure is being challenged in several states, including California, where the two largest AAA clubs are located. Proxy fights there and in Michigan and Connecticut have brought some limited reforms despite the clubs' refusal to give challengers access to membership lists.

AAA members can help revitalize their automobile clubs if they realize how good the AAA could be. For example, the best AAA affiliate—the Auto Club of Missouri—runs an automotive diagnostic clinic to examine members' cars and specify exactly what repairs are needed. After repairs have been made, the clinic will recheck the car to make sure they were done and done correctly. Time after time, the clinic has found members charged for new parts when they received used ones or none at all. And the clinic often finds that a minor adjustment or repair will do when service stations and franchise auto dealers try to sell members repairs costing hundreds of dollars. The Missouri club's St. Louis clinic has been so successful—it has been operating in the black for three years now—that a second one is being opened in Kansas City to serve members in the western part of the state. Every medium-to-large-sized club should be urged to follow the example of Missouri and open such a clinic. They can be built for less than $250,000 and should be making money within two years of operation. AAA clubs could also sponsor group legal services for warranty, accident, or traffic violation cases. Of real value would be a national task force sponsored by the AAA to better the owner's warranty position in relation to the manufacturer or dealer. Member clubs can easily organize their own automobile safety and complaint centers (see page 63). Finally, the AAA, nationally and locally, could use its considerable political resources to lobby for tougher automobile safety standards, safer highway construction, expanded mass transit and stronger laws to control pollution.

To move clubs to action, AAA members must demand that their club executives and directors respond to members' needs. Whenever an auto consumer problem is reported locally, members should ask AAA officials—in letters either directly to them, or to the editors of their local newspapers—what AAA is doing about it. Both Michigan and North Carolina newspapers, for example, conducted lengthy investigations of illegal but widespread odometer tampering by used car dealers. The Carolina and Michigan AAAs ignored the problem; AAA members should have asked why publicly. The U.S. Department of Transportation frequently delays requiring recalls of cars with defective parts. Defective motor mounts on Chevrolets and lower control arms on Fords are the most glaring recent examples. AAA members should ask their club leaders—through letters to their local newspapers—what AAA has done to help solve this problem. When recalls are announced, members should find out what their clubs are doing to make sure all owners of defective cars are notified. And when the manufacturers delay, refuse to make repairs, or demand payment for ones already made—problems that are much too common—AAA members should demand aid from their clubs, and let the local newspapers know when AAA does or doesn't help.

Besides publicity, AAA members should find out when their local AAA club holds its annual membership meeting, if there is one. Short of waging a full-fledged proxy fight, members should attend to ask club officials what they're doing about consumer problems. Such meetings are also a good time to get press coverage, to help inform other AAA members about what AAA is failing to do on their behalf.

Finally, even AAA clubs that don't have membership meetings will have boards of directors or advisory boards. These directors and advisers are often local business and government notables, often unaware of the many things AAA could be doing. Members should write to their club directors or confront them personally to persuade them to take an interest in auto-oriented consumer protection activities.

The ultimate sanction against indifferent club directors is to remove them by means of proxy fights. Such proxy fights have been conducted against the three largest clubs —northern and southern California and Michigan—and two smaller ones—North Jersey and Hartford, Connecticut, with some modest innovations produced so far. Litigation has been started against other clubs, including Chicago, in attempts to get information from close-mouthed club officials who in some cases refuse even to give their members the club's by-laws.

The member clubs of the AAA have the potential to become consumer champions, but only if members achieve reform. It is well worth the effort. A small fraction of the club's estimated $300 million annual dues (not to mention other assets and their profits from insurance, travel, and equipment sales, estimated to total $1.5 billion annually) could form an automobile owner's lobby capable of matching muscle with the Big Three auto manufacturers. Such a lobby working on the local, state, and federal levels could begin to end the domination of isolated, helpless consumers by united, powerful dealers and manufacturers.

How to Do a Bank Interest Survey

At one time only large purchases like housing or automobiles were bought on credit. Now credit is a way of life. Banks, loan companies, credit unions, and others compete with one another for a larger share of the consumer installment debt. For home mortgages, the principal sources are savings and loan associations, mutual savings banks, life insurance companies, and commercial banks.

The interest charged by these firms varies. It is in the consumer's interest to find the cheapest credit source. Even if it means only a small reduction on the single monthly payments, it can become significant when the saving is multiplied by 24 or 36 months. To realize the greatest saving, the consumer must compare the credit charges of various companies. There are a number of ways that these charges are expressed.

Most consumers are familiar with the usual advertising devices— "only a few pennies a day," or "only a few dollars per month," or "interest charges of only 1.5 percent per month." Less familiar are the implications of figuring interest by "add-on" or "discount" methods. For example, with the add-on method you would borrow $3,000 for 3 years, but, at 10 percent interest, have to pay back $3,400. With the discount method, you would sign a note for $3,350 but receive a check for $3,000 because $350 charge is taken out in advance.

The problem is that these methods offer the consumer no basis for comparison. Is it less costly to borrow a few pennies a day or a few dollars a month? How does a 9 percent add-on rate compare to an 18 percent annual rate? For the vast majority of consumers, these are comparisons between apples and oranges. They make no sense at all.

To help prevent such confusion, Congress passed the Consumer Credit Protection Act of 1968 (popularly known as the Truth-in-Lending law). The purpose of the act is

to assure a meaningful disclosure of credit terms so that the consumer will be able to compare more readily the various credit terms available to him and to avoid the uninformed use of credit.

The Truth-in-Lending law recognized that the only way for a consumer to discover what credit really costs is to establish a uniform means of measurement—to compare apples with apples. The Truth-in-Lending law thus requires that all interest rates be quoted according to the *annual percentage rate* of interest. Of course, the interest costs must also be quoted to consumers *before* loans are actually made. This means that all credit advertising must "state the rate of that charge expressed as an annual percentage rate."

Surveys in several cities have indicated that this standard is not being obeyed. For example, a telephone survey of 223 banks in Cleveland, conducted by the Ohio Public Interest Action Group, revealed that 87 banks—almost two out of five—did not mention the annual percentage rate as required by the Truth-in-Lending law. A bare quarter of the Cleveland banks quoted only the annual percentage rate. The rest were not in actual violation of the law, although they confused consumers by quoting both monthly and annual rates.

Citizens have three remedies against this kind of deception: administrative, civil, and criminal. At the very least, public complaints to the offending lending institution, accompanied by letters to the appropriate regulatory agency, can often help to change a deceptive policy. The Comptroller of the Currency (Mr. William Camp, Treasury Department, 15th and New York Avenue, N.W., Washington, D.C. 20220), regulates national banks; the Federal Reserve Board (20th and Constitution, Washington, D.C. 20551) regulates member state banks; and the Federal Deposit Insurance Corporation (FDIC) (550 17th Street, N.W., Washington, D.C. 20429), along with your state banking commissioner, regulates insured banks which are neither national nor within the Federal Reserve System. Loan companies are usually regulated, if at all, by a state official whose title varies from state to state. Federal savings and loan associations are regulated by the Federal Home Loan Bank Board (101 Indiana Avenue, N.W., Washington, D.C. 20552).

Additionally, courts have always allowed civil action for those who were injured financially by bank deception. Some courts have held that the purpose of the Consumer Credit Protection Act was "to create a species of private attorney generals to participate prominently in enforcement," whether or not the party himself was actually financially injured or deceived. This means that citizen investigators who uncover fraud may be able on their own to recover civil penalties against offending banks. Criminal charges may also be brought by a U.S. attorney if there has been a knowing, willful violation of the act.

A citizen investigation aimed at discovering which institutions are violating the law can be conducted by means of a telephone survey of all the banks within an area. The findings of that survey can be compiled into a short report, which should be released to the press and all concerned parties.

To form a valid comparison among banks, accuracy and adherence to a set formula are important. The survey form below, adapted from one used by the Retired Professionals Action Group in their Washington, D.C., bank survey, will help guarantee accuracy and will give citizen investigators a standard measure of comparison for annual interest rate quotations. It can also be used for questioning finance companies on rates alone. For home mortgages, a considerable revision of the form will be needed to cover additional fees customarily exacted in such a loan.

RETIRED PROFESSIONALS ACTION GROUP
INTEREST RATE SURVEY

1. Name of caller _____

2. Date call was made _____
   Name of bank called _____
   Location of branch called _____
   Phone number used _____

3. "Hello, may I please speak to somebody about getting a new car loan? Thank you." (Phone call transferred to new person.)

4. "With whom am I speaking, please?" (Name of person answering) _____
   "What is your position?" _____

5. Do you know about the cost of a new-car loan from your bank?" ____ Answer should be yes; if not, get

transferred to someone who says yes, and enter new name in answer to 4.

6. "Well then, I am buying a new Chevrolet Impala and I need to borrow $3,500 to buy the car, repayable in three years. Could you please tell me what rate you charge for this kind of loan?"

    Answer received (a) _____

    (Enter as given) (b) _____

    (c) _____

7. If the following information is not given in answer to 6, then ask, "Thank you, but what will the monthly payment be that I will have to make?" $_____

    "What will the total amount be over and above the $3,500 that I'll have to pay? I'd like to know that."

    Answer $_____

8. "Do the figures that you've quoted include credit life insurance?" _____ (yes or no)

9. "What is the rate including credit life insurance?" _____

    _____

10. "If I can get the credit life insurance cheaper, can I supply it myself?" _____

11. "Is what you have told me all I need to know?" _____

    _____

12. If the information is not already given, and if the answer to Question 11 has not produced the information, then say, "Oh, by the way, you said the interest was _____ add-on (or _____ discount, as the case may be), what is that rate in terms of an annual percentage rate on the true basis, on outstanding balances?"

    _____

Conclude by saying, "Thank you very much, you have helped me a lot in deciding what to do, and I do appreciate very much the time you have given me. Good-bye!"

How to Help Savings and Loan Associations Serve the Public Interest

Savings and loan associations are the third largest repository of money in the United States. Their combined assets total over two hundred billion dollars. To the average citizen, savings and loan associations (S&Ls) look and act like banks. People deposit money in them and the money earns interest. In turn, they can borrow money on which they have to pay interest. But in several important ways, S&Ls are different from banks.

First, most S&Ls are owned by the depositors. All but 695 of the more than 5,000 associations are mutually owned—the members of the association own it in common. They exercise direction through an elected board of directors. Another important difference stems from their origins. Savings and loan associations were formed by members of immigrant groups pooling their savings for mutual benefit. Unlike corporations, which tie voting rights to the amount of the investment, S&Ls give proportionally greater weight to the small shareholder than to the large. In federally chartered * S&Ls, each depositor of $5 gets one vote, but no matter how many thousands of dollars are deposited, the largest shareholder gets no more than fifty votes.

Because of their origins, and the fact that traditionally S&Ls are supposed to benefit the community in which the association is located, they are limited almost exclusively to financing residential structures. At the end of 1971, about

* There are both state and federal S&Ls. The rules governing them are similar, but for uniformity this project deals only with federal S&Ls.

84.5 percent of their total savings balances were invested in loans on homes or apartments. Almost 75 percent of all mortgage loans held by insured associations financed single-family homes.

These characteristics are important to citizens interested in bettering their own communities. For example, if an S&L located in an inner city invests only in suburban housing, then, in effect, the poor are financing the homes of the rich and accelerating the deterioration of the city. In a college town, an S&L which receives most of its business from students may refuse to invest in off-campus student housing. These policies are responsive neither to the depositors nor to the communities in which the association is located.

Theoretically, because members are owners, they should be able to change the composition of the board and thus change association policy. In practice this has not worked. The reason is that most depositors do not realize they are also the owners of the association. Of those who realize it, most don't care in part because they do not know what their combined power can do. A determined citizens group can change this attitude.

The first step after joining an S&L is to study the association's by-laws carefully. Step two is to discover what investment policies the association follows. An interview with an officer of the association should raise pointed questions about the criteria used to determine investments, where most investments are made, and whether the association has a commitment to social action.

If the officer refuses to answer or is evasive, it may be possible to find out where the association has invested its money by examining the mortgagee index. The indices are public information and are available for inspection at the office of the county clerk or the recorder of deeds. If the county doesn't keep mortgagee information, all mortgage books for a period of years would have to be searched to make up a list of mortgage loans by a particular S&L. Another, though less satisfactory, means of finding out about the S&Ls policies, is to enlist the cooperation of an inner city and a suburban homeowner who can serve as a test case to gauge the association's reaction. Each owner can ask for mortgage money and the results may give an indication of the association's attitude. Be careful, however, because the test may be affected by factors unrelated to discriminatory policies.

If it can be determined that the association is unresponsive to community needs and uninterested in instituting reforms, step three is to launch a campaign against the policies of the present board of directors. The best way to do this is by means of a proxy fight at the next election of board officers. All federal (and most state) S&Ls elect directors at the annual meeting held in the afternoon of the third Wednesday of January. Be sure to check the by-laws for precise information about how the reform slate of directors can be nominated. Most S&Ls require written nominations, signed by a specified number of members, to be filed in advance of the meeting.

A distinguished reform slate will be a great help in soliciting your proxies. Avoid proposing directors who will have a potential conflict-of-interest, i.e., real estate brokers, title insurance people, bankers, property insurance people, and appraisers of real estate. Instead, propose strong community leaders who will be knowledgeable about credit matters. Particularly impressive are professors or teachers of economics, credit managers of substantial businesses, heads of successful businesses in the community, and credit union managers. Also excellent are officers of civic associations and citizens groups, youth leaders, clergymen, and attorneys who do not have a large real estate practice.

In addition to a slate of directors, your reform campaign should have a platform upon which to campaign. Some possibilities are the following, all of them reforms achievable in one year:

1. Amend by-laws to provide for annual solicitation of proxies for each annual meeting, the solicitation to be

made by a "proxy statement" similar to those of other public businesses.

2. Give each member annually a proper statement of earnings in the same detail that other publicly owned businesses must send to shareholders, with disclosure of the top five salaries paid.

3. Require all residential (one–four family) mortgages to be drawn up exclusively on the approved Federal Home Loan Mortgage Corporation form with no side agreements that may diminish the consumers' rights.

4. Prohibit all directors from receiving fees in connection with any mortgage transaction with the association for appraisals, brokerage, insurance, legal fees, or commissions on title insurance. All fees which may legally be collected should be collected for the association itself.

5. Prohibit all directors and all salaried officials from receiving any compensation, owning stock, or receiving anything of value from any service corporation having any contract with the association.

To wage a credible proxy fight with any chance of success, several things must be done. First, the campaign must begin at least four months before the January meeting. It takes a substantial amount of time to put together a winning effort. Second, a proxy form and opposition slate must be selected. It is important that the proxy be drawn in accordance with legal requirements and that only eligible candidates be chosen. Third, an attempt should be made to obtain a list of all depositors. The list is important because many associations secure proxies from members when they open their accounts; when new depositors go to open an account they are handed both signature cards and a proxy statement, printed in microscopic type. Most sign without hesitation. This backlog of signed cards gives management a tremendous advantage in any proxy contest, unless members are willing to revoke their proxies and turn over new ones to the insurgents. Board members will usually resist attempts to get the list of depositors, but the by-laws of some associations require that the list be made available. State corporation law may grant the same right.

Even if the list cannot be obtained, there are other ways to help even the odds. Interested groups of students, church congregations, clubs, and individuals can be urged to open accounts and turn over their proxies to the reform group. This tactic is especially useful in university towns, where large numbers of depositors can be mobilized. Be sure to check the by-laws to determine the date before which the deposit must be made for the new member to qualify to vote at the meeting. Newspaper advertisements soliciting proxies can be helpful. A second tactic is to station presentable and articulate proxy collectors in the lobby or on the street outside each branch of the association to explain the reform effort and to attempt to get depositors to revoke their management proxies or to sign over a new proxy to the reform group. Local ordinances should be checked to see if a permit is necessary to solicit in this manner. As a last resort, a suit might be filed asking the court to discard management proxies obtained by deceptive tactics. For example, if depositors are told that they *must* sign the proxy statement to open an account, they are being unjustly coerced into giving away a vital membership right. A court might well hold that all proxies obtained in such a fashion are invalid.

Step four, of course, is to encourage as much media coverage as possible during the campaign and at the annual meeting. Proper publicity puts pressure on management and helps to recruit new allies.

Step five is to be ready to negotiate. After all, the main purpose of the campaign is to make the association responsive to community needs. If the present directors see that the citizens group is both determined and capable of making a serious fight, they may be willing to give in to many of the reformers' arguments rather than face bad publicity and run the risk of actually losing a proxy battle.

Two additional points need to be made in connection

with a proxy contest. Be sure to caution those who give proxies to the reform group *not* to sign any further management proxies. When apprised of a fight, management may obtain a new proxy with each deposit slip or other transaction. In a proxy fight, the *latest dated* proxy wins. Second, if the fight is so close that votes have to be counted at the annual meeting, urge depositors to show up at the meeting, revoke their proxies, and vote in person. An oral revocation at the meeting is ordinarily sufficient. Again, check the by-laws. Also be sure to request that an independent teller be appointed to count the votes.

There have not been many proxy contests to require S&Ls to be more socially responsive. One that was waged unsuccessfully occurred in Washington, D.C., during late 1969 and 1970. The Jews for Urban Justice, a group of young Jewish activists, learned that Guardian Federal Savings and Loan Association was not investing money in poorer areas of the district, but instead was concentrating investments in upper-middle-class white neighborhoods. JUJ started its campaign only six weeks before the annual meeting and failed in its attempt to get the membership list. The only tactic used was to solicit proxies from depositors entering or leaving one of the Guardian's six branches. Given the shortage of time, inability to obtain the list, and coverage of only one out of six branches, the campaign failed and in the end only 899 votes out of 62,600 votes cast supported JUJ candidates. Nevertheless, management was shaken and agreed to some insurgent proposals, including appointing JUJ members to an advisory board. A stronger, better organized campaign undoubtedly could have negotiated more concessions.

A lesson to be learned from the JUJ experience is that ill-financed, badly timed campaigns cannot hope to succeed against large S&Ls in urban areas. Much less organization is needed for a campaign against a small town S&L, especially if a large campus is located nearby. Instead of concentrating exclusively on a proxy contest involving only present depositors, insurgents can persuade hundreds of new members to join the association. After all, it costs little to join and any money that is deposited will earn interest. These new members joined by old depositors might be able to muster strength sufficient to reform an S&L. One victory would breathe new vitality into the concept of community control of S&Ls and serve as a warning to other S&Ls that unless they become responsive, they may face a losing battle to retain control of the association.

A threat to this strategy lies in a plan by the Federal Home Loan Bank Board, the government agency which regulates S&Ls, to issue regulations permitting them to convert from mutual associations to stock corporations. Some economic advantages might be obtained by such a move. But one certain result would be concentration of voting control in the hands of large depositors who would receive shares proportional to their deposits. Small shareholders would effectively be frozen out of the decision-making process. This policy goes against the history of S&Ls and ignores the benefits of mutual ownership, which distributes control to a more representative cross-section of the community.

The Citizen Action Group intends to oppose any regulations that remove S&Ls from community control. CAG will provide further information and assistance to citizen groups opposing conversions of S&Ls from mutual associations to stock corporations. Write Citizen Action Group, 2000 P Street, N.W., Washington, D.C. 20036, and Representative Wright Patman, House Banking and Currency Committee, House of Representatives, Washington, D.C.

How to Evaluate Pension Funds

The pension project is unlike most other projects in this manual. The others focus on ways in which an individual

or groups of individuals working in concert can better the
society in which they live. The focus of the pension project,
by contrast, is on ways individuals can directly protect
themselves. Of course, if pensions could be reformed across
the board, millions of workers would benefit. But due to
the present overwhelming inequities in various laws, the
best way to reform pensions is not to set out to help
workers nationally, but for individuals, union locals, and
citizen groups to protect themselves. Hundreds of con-
frontations over pension rights and benefits will build up
pressure for national reform. And it is only through a
sweeping reform of the pension laws that many of the
problems described in this section can be solved.

Most people never think seriously about pensions until
retirement draws near. By then, it is usually too late. Although 34 million Americans are enrolled in private pension
plans, Senator Jacob Javits estimates that as few as one
in twelve employees who have enrolled in plans during
their careers will ultimately receive pension benefits. Even
professional pension managers, not noted for their pessi-
mism, estimate that only half of those enrolled in plans
will actually collect benefits.

One common reason that people lose their pension rights
is that they aren't informed about their plan's requirements:
how old they must be to earn a benefit, for example, or how
many years they must work for the same employer. As a
result, after twenty or thirty years of work, they find that
because of a technicality they were unaware of, they fail
to qualify for pension benefits.

In other cases, people lose benefits because of circumstances beyond their control. Lay-offs, for example, are a
frequent cause of pension loss; lay-offs become particularly
damaging when they occur a few months or years before
the pension is due to "vest," that is, before the benefits
become nonforfeitable. When a plant closes down or a
company is sold, employees often lose pension benefits.
The same thing happens when an employee changes jobs.
Even a move from one union local to another within the

same union may cost an employee his pension rights. The right to a pension can also be lost *after* retirement, if for any reason a plan terminates or goes broke.

Thus, for most employees, a pension is not the sure thing they thought it was, but a gamble against long odds. The odds are better for certain employees than for others. In general, it is far easier for managerial employees to meet pension requirements. For one thing, they change jobs with less frequency than lower-level white-collar and blue-collar workers, which means they run less risk of losing their pensions and also get larger benefits. The result is that those who need it least are protected best.

Citizens who are not enrolled in a private pension plan should also be concerned about this problem because the public ultimately picks up the tab for a private pension system that approaches a national fraud. Each year private pensions receive a tax subsidy of more than three billion dollars. Employers do not pay taxes on their contributions to pension plans and earnings from the $180 billion invested in private pension plans go untaxed. And because private pensions exclude so many of the neediest in the retired population, social security benefits and welfare assistance must constantly increase and the public pays the bill. Finally, manufacturers use their payments to pension plans as an excuse to raise consumer prices.

For those who are covered, the time to investigate a pension plan is *not* when retirement is imminent. An employee should investigate the plan at the time it is proposed or at the time he joins the plan. The following questions provide a framework for a study of a pension plan.

1. What will you get from the pension plan: (a) if you quit your job today; (b) if you work under the plan until retirement?

2. How is the size of your benefits determined? Is it a fixed benefit? Does it depend on the number of years worked? On years worked plus salary over your entire career? On your salary in the years of highest pay, or during the last five or ten years of employment?

3. Might you lose your pension: (a) if you leave the company; (b) if you change unions or union locals; (c) if you are laid off for a certain period of time?

4. Will your years worked before the plan was established count toward a pension?

5. How many people currently employed under the plan are expected to receive a pension?

6. If you are under a multi-employer plan, what companies and unions are part of the plan?

7. Under any kind of plan, are there reciprocity agreements that will allow you to change jobs and carry your credits with you? If so, what industries and unions are involved and where are they located?

8. Does your plan offer a survivor's benefit? Is it optional? If so, how do you go about choosing a survivor's benefit? Does the employer contribute anything to help pay for the survivor's benefit?

9. Does your plan include cost-of-living provisions? Does it offer "equity annuity" provisions allowing you to gear part of the contributions made on your behalf to the stock market?

10. How do you apply for a pension: (a) if you retire while still working under the plan; (b) if you leave the company before you have retired?

12. What happens if the plan terminates? Is the plan insured? Will there be enough money for everyone? Will benefits be paid only to those with nonforfeitable vested benefit rights? Will they be paid only to employees who are already retired or over age sixty? If there is not enough money for everyone, what will you get?

13. Does your employer make regular contributions to the pension fund or does he pay benefits as qualified workers retire? Have the contributions increased or decreased recently?

14. If the employer makes regular contributions, do they cover credits earned before the plan was set up?

15. At what date will the plan have enough money on hand to cover all credits?

16. Who administers your plan? That is, who decides which employees qualify for benefits, and who authorizes payments of benefits? (This is usually a pension board which may be comprised of corporate officers, or of management and union officials. Sometimes, third-party representatives are appointed to the pension board.)

17. Who takes care of the money? That is, who is legally responsible as fund trustee for management of the funds that are supposed to pay you a benefit? A bank? An insurance company? Several financial institutions, such as banks, insurance companies, and investment firms?

18. Does the employer or pension board have any control over investment of the funds by the trustee?

19. How are the funds invested? How do trustees exercise their proxy voting power? Do they consult beneficiaries in purchasing stock and in voting their shares?

20. What is the rate of earnings?

21. How much money is going into administration of the plan?

An employee should be able to get the answers to all of these questions. If an employer refuses to cooperate, the list of questions and an affidavit describing his refusal should be sent to the Assistant Secretary of Labor, Labor Management Services Administration, Department of Labor, Room 3137, 14th and Constitution Avenue, N.W., Washington, D.C. 20210. Copies should also be sent to the Senate Labor Committee and the House General Labor Subcommittee, Capitol Hill, Washington, D.C.

There is much that government, unions, and associations of employees can do to protect employee pension rights. The important fact to remember is that the time for citizen action is now, before millions more retire only to find that the pension promise was a mirage. For more details about the private pension problem and what you can do about it, see *You and Your Pension,* a new book by Ralph Nader and Kate Blackwell (Grossman, 1973).

Consuming Television:
The Citizen's Role in Cable TV

Cable television had humble beginnings. The first system was installed in 1952 to bring TV to viewers whose reception of over-the-air signals was blocked by high mountains. By installing master antennae on mountain tops, cable operators were able to feed TV signals by coaxial cable to subscribers living in valley towns. Because there were no buildings, mountains, or other obstacles to interfere with cable signals, "ghosts" and static were eliminated and reception was far superior to over-the-air broadcasts. Besides clearer pictures, cable offered other advantages. Over-the-air broadcasting is limited to reception of 12 channels, 2 through 13. Cable systems transmit 12 to 40 channels, permitting greater program diversity. (Proposed Federal Communication Commission rules require all new systems to have at least 20 stations.) Because cable is supported by monthly charges, averaging about $5.00 per set, cable operators are not dependent on advertising. Those that do accept commercials charge on the average only $88 for an hour-long program, far less than the cost of even the cheapest over-the-air rates.

Today cable is in the midst of a tremendous expansion. Nearly five million people, mostly in small- and medium-sized towns, are serviced by about 2,800 cable systems. Another 1,950 systems are approved but not yet constructed and 2,400 franchise applications are pending before local governments. Subscriber lists are increasing at a rate of 20 percent per year. The cable industry predicts that by 1980, thirty million homes will be hooked into cable systems. By the end of the century over-the-air broadcasting will be almost completely eliminated.

The potential of a nationwide cable network is nothing short of fantastic. The Office of Communication of the United Church of Christ notes that cable can:

1. Provide local news and information about what's going on in the town, the community, the neighborhood—even the block.
2. Make it possible for community organizations to conduct meetings in which cable viewers participate via the home screen. A cable system may be subdivided into smaller units such as political wards, school districts, or ethnic community areas. It is possible for cable systems to permit two-way communication, letting an individual at home express opinions on community issues by means of a signaling device on the television set. Ultimately there will be provisions for talk-back.
3. Make it possible for you to "sit in" regularly on public meetings such as the town council or the board of education.
4. Make it possible for the board of education to distribute televised adult education courses in to the home, or to teach children at home if they are physically unable to go to school. Community colleges can offer course work, too.
5. Make it possible, at very low cost, for candidates for elected office at various levels of government to discuss issues of interest to their constituents.
6. Provide "public access"—the opportunity for individuals and organizations to speak their minds on whatever they think important.●

There will be social and entertainment benefits as well. Shoppers will be able to pick out and order merchandise from their own living rooms. Mail and newspapers can be delivered by cable. Two-way response mechanisms will permit viewer participation.

Whether these abilities are used to serve the public interest will depend in large part on the citizen response to the challenge of cable. Back in the 1920s people dreamed that radio would emerge as a force for public good. In the 1940s the same dreams were spun when television began

● *A Short Course in Cable*, Office of Communications, United Church of Christ, June 1972.

to be developed commercially. Needless to say, neither dream was realized, as commercial considerations quickly overwhelmed public service possibilities. If the same fate is not to overcome cable, citizens must act now.

The first step is to learn what cable can do. The Federal Communications Commission (FCC) sets standards for cable operation. A copy of the proposed FCC standards on cable may be obtained by writing to the Federal Communications Commission, 1919 M Street, N.W., Washington, D.C. 20554. Federal standards are supplemented by agreements worked out locally between the cable operator and area governments. It is at the local level where citizens can exert the greatest impact. A good explanation of cable can be found in "The Wired Nation," by Ralph Lee Smith, *The Nation*, May 18, 1970 (copies will be distributed by *The Nation*, 333 Sixth Avenue, New York, N.Y. 10014; minimum order 10 copies for $3.00). The best guides for citizen action are two United Church of Christ publications: *Cable Television: A Guide for Citizen Action*, by Monroe Price and John Wicklein, Pilgrim Press, $2.95; and *A Short Course in Cable*, free, 12 pages. Both are obtainable from the Office of Communications, United Church of Christ, 289 Park Avenue South, New York, N.Y. 10010. Problems of local franchising are described in *Crossed Wires*, a report by the Center for the Analysis of Public Issues, 92A Nassau Street, Princeton, N.J. 08540 ($5.00).

The basic question of cable is how the benefits should be shared. Communities give cable operators a franchise to develop a system for an entire community or for a particular section of a large city. A franchise is nothing more than a contract, the provisions of which are subject to negotiations among the cable operator, local government and concerned citizens. Depending on the relative strengths of each party to the negotiations, a contract will be drawn which is fair or which tips the balance in favor of one set or another of interests.

It is important that citizens themselves participate in these negotiations and that they do not complacently rely on government. Too often local officials are satisfied if an operator provides government with access to one or two channels and a small share of the revenues. Sometimes government cooperation is purchased by cutting officials in on a share of the profits. Other times local officials are too busy to learn the potential of cable. Whether out of ignorance or avarice, the result is the same: a franchise is approved that does not provide maximum benefits for citizens.

Because of the rapid expansion of cable, most areas either have already granted franchises or will be entering into franchise negotiations in the near future. Citizens can play an important role in either situation, though it is best to participate in the negotiations for the franchise agreement. If a franchise has already been granted and the operators performance is unsatisfactory in terms of service, type of programming, or speed of construction of the system, the first step citizen activists should take is to obtain a copy of the franchise agreement and study it carefully. If possible, a lawyer should be enlisted to help analyze the duty of the operator and the rights of citizens. Every franchise has performance requirements which the operator has agreed to fulfill. Some franchises specify that construction of the system must begin within a certain period of time. Others require the operator to keep up with technological improvements to give the city the best service possible. Failure to live up to these or other agreements means that the operator has not lived up to his side of the franchise agreement. If the breach is serious there probably are provisions for fines or cancellation of the franchise.

Even if the operator is living up to the terms of the agreement, citizens may still be dissatisfied. Many franchises were negotiated by government officials who knew little about the potential of cable. As a result they required only minimal performance by the operator. Unfortunately, the possibilities for citizen action in such a case are limited. If the franchise agreement is non-exclusive, citizens may be able to persuade government officials to grant a new franchise to a competing operator. Even if it proves impossible to recruit a new operator, the threat of competition may itself be sufficient to improve service. Another tactic is to mobilize public opinion in an attempt to persuade the operator to modify the agreement voluntarily. Meetings, petitions, and citizen hearings can be employed to educate the public and to build support for modifications. Finally, if the operator remains recalcitrant and the issue is serious, citizens may attempt to persuade existing customers to discontinue service and dissuade new customers from signing up.

If the cable operator wishes to raise rates, a public hearing usually must be held. Citizens can intervene in the hearings to tie a rate increase to improved performance. Mergers can also be used as a leverage point to move operators to action. Because operators must receive municipal approval for a merger, citizens have an opportunity to demand that officials require improved performance or block the merger.

Once a franchise has been granted, citizens have an uphill struggle to win better terms. But before the agreement is finalized much can be done to shape it in a way that citizens will be benefited. Individuals can exert some influence by mastering the intricacies of cable and convincing government officials of the need to guarantee citizen rights. But to be truly effective, citizens must join together to counter the pressure that is certain to be exerted by the cable operator. (See page 213 for directions on how to form a citizen action club.)

The type of service that an area will receive will largely depend on the terms of the franchise that is negotiated. The following checklist indicates some of the more important steps to be taken and rights to be secured.

1. The previous record of an applicant for a cable franchise should be checked thoroughly. Often speculators buy up franchises hoping to make a profit by selling out to another operator. Check to see whether the applicant for your community's franchise has lived up to his promises elsewhere.

2. One channel should be reserved for educational use,

one for governmental use and two for public, non-profit, non-commercial users. One or two additional channels should be made open-access channels at no cost to anyone who wishes to use them. At least one other channel should be held in reserve so that later, when cable is more fully developed, it will be available for uses which now are still not known. The FCC has said that it favors reserving half the channels on any system to be used for non-entertainment programming.

3. A franchise agreement should require the operator to use the most modern equipment possible and to improve the system as technological advances become available.

4. The FCC has required "two way" capability in systems operating in the top one hundred markets. In smaller communities, this requirement can be written into the franchise by the local franchising body.

5. The term of the franchise should never exceed fifteen years. Ten years would seem to be a more reasonable length of time. Radio and television presently receive only three-year licenses.

6. Provisions should be made to require construction of the system within a definite period of time. No merger or sale of the franchise should be permitted without prior government approval.

7. Radio signals from distant cities can be carried on cable. Bringing in signals from other parts of the world or from other countries would be a way of enhancing the flow of information to a community. The franchise can require the operator to provide this service.

8. Other provisions to serve the public interest can also be written in. For example, the operator could be required to maintain a studio and equipment, fixed and portable, so that citizens can produce their own shows. Definite amounts of programming time for local news, sports, and local talent shows can be required.

The most important point to remember is that once the franchise is set unless the cable operator breaks the agreement it is difficult to alter the terms. Therefore, in communities where cable systems have not yet been franchised, citizens should organize themselves early to ensure that the most favorable provisions possible are adopted. Remember that, in a contest between a wealthy operator and citizens with few resources, the latter have little chance of securing their rights unless they organize.

Shedding the Light: How to Preserve Natural Resources and Save Taxpayers' Money

For the average citizen, the energy crisis is baffling and complex. Coal, oil, gas, hydroelectric power, and atomic sources of energy seem to be either in short supply, too costly, or environmentally hazardous. It is not the purpose of this project to attempt to unravel all the complexities of the energy crisis. Instead, it focuses on one use of electric power: lighting in schools, hospitals, and commercial buildings.

The demand for electric power has been growing at the incredible rate of 9 percent per year, almost double the rate of growth of all other energy forms. By 1990, new transmission lines alone will cover three million acres of land—an area equivalent in size to the entire state of Connecticut.

Lighting is an important part of our electric power consumption. It accounts for $7 billion of electric bills per year. General Electric's calculations show that 24 percent of all electric power goes into lighting and that in some urban areas, lighting accounts for up to 65 percent of the electrical load. In new office buildings constructed according to the most recent *minimum* lighting standards, 50 to 60 percent of the total electric requirements go for lighting.

Lighting standards are promulgated by a "lighting lobby" consisting of power and utility companies, light fixture firms, and industry groups such as the Edison Electric Institute, the Better Light, Better Sight Bureau, and the Illuminating Engineering Society—all of which have a vested interest in increasing power consumption or lighting equipment sales. The success of this lobby in boosting lighting levels has been phenomenal. From 1910 to the present, the recommended standard for general interior lighting has risen 2,000 percent. The average level of light in commercial buildings has tripled, from 40 foot-candles in 1940 to 125 foot-candles in 1972.* An IES study predicts that the level will double, to 250 foot-candles by the year 2000. In 1930, the level of recommended lighting provided 90 percent visual accuracy at levels that today would be about one-fifth of the prescribed light level *minimums*. Successive foot-candle increases provide only marginal increases in visibility at a steadily increasing cost to consumers and to the environment.

Lighting in schools provides a good example of these exponential increases. In 1919 the Illuminating Engineering Society's standards for classroom illumination was set at 3 foot-candles. That figure rose to 5 foot-candles by 1943 and to 30 foot-candles by 1952. The 1972 level is between 70 and 100 candles. By comparison, the level for British schools remains at only 10 foot-candles. British scientists contend this level provides 90 percent visual accuracy, a comfortable level for reading. To move to a 98 percent accuracy level would require a tenfold increase in the foot-candle level. The British feel the slight improvement, which in not significant in terms of efficiency or health, is not worth the increased cost.

Before describing what can be done to limit increases in lighting levels, it is important to dispel the common mis-

* One foot-candle is equal to the light of one candle at a distance of one foot.

conception that better light equals better sight. Obviously it is possible to see more in daylight than in darkness and up to a point bright light gives more visibility than dim light. But better light does *not* produce better eyesight, nor does dim light produce worse eyesight. The myth that better light equals better sight has been foisted on the public by various lobbyists with economic interests in raising illumination levels. The "Better Light, Better Sight" Bureau's name itself feeds the myth. Medical evidence does not support the lighting lobby's contention. Dr. David G. Logan writing in the *New England Journal of Medicine* (Vol. 224) stated: "There is no generally acceptable evidence that poor illumination results in organic harm to the eyes any more than indistinct sound damages the ears or faint smells damage the nose." This opinion is shared by most other experts. Dr. Howard N. Bernstein, M.D., Director of Ocular Research of the Washington Hospital Center, in a May 25, 1972, letter to the Public Interest Research Group stated three points:

1. The level of illumination only needs to be adequate enough to permit performance of the task without undue strain or discomfort. This, of course, will vary with the circumstances.

2. Too little illumination has never been shown to produce any harm to the eyes. . . .

3. On the other hand, excessive illumination can potentially be harmful.

Richard G. Stein writing in *Environment Magazine* in October, 1972, concludes: "It appears that adequate lighting could be installed in institutions, commercial buildings, schools and so forth with less than 50 percent of present light loads." Stein cites evidence from M. A. Tinker's work during the 1930s that 10 to 15 foot-candles should be enough light for reading when one's eyes are normal and print is legible. (For further information on Tinker's work in this area, see M. A. Tinker's, "The Effect of Illumination Intensities upon Fatigue in Reading," *Journal of Educational Psychology*, 1939.) More recent experiments, conducted in

1968 by P. C. Butler and J. J. Rusmore at San Jose State College, indicate that levels between 3 and 10 foot-candles are adequate for efficient reading (P. C. Butler and J. J. Rusmore, *Perceptual and Motor Skills,* 1969).

A citizen activist can arouse concern about excessive lighting from several perspectives. To the environmentalist, more lighting requires more energy which in turn causes more pollution. To the consumer, more light means more expense. To the taxpayer, higher lighting levels mean greater maintenance expenses in public buildings. According to Keyes Metcalf, a highly respected library consultant, increasing the illumination levels of a 90,000-square-foot building from a reasonable 25- to 50-foot-candle level to the 90- to 105-foot-candle level recommended by IES would increase the annual lighting bill from approximately $11,000 to over $27,000.

Even though the cost per foot-candle is less today than in the past, consumers are paying far more since far more foot-candles are being used. General Electric claims that "the cost of lighting has gone down 30 percent since 1958," but fails to mention that illumination levels have risen almost 70 percent—which more than cancels any savings.

To help cut back on both taxpayer expense and environmental pollution, the citizen activist must first discover what formal lighting standards, if any, exist in his community. Sometimes standards are actually written into statutes or are imposed by building regulations or health and safety codes governing schools, hospitals, or other public buildings. A phone call to the chief architect or engineer responsible for school or hospital construction or to the local building code inspector will usually yield the desired information.

The next step, if formal standards exist, is to discover how they were adopted. Frequently, standards were simply transferred to the municipal or state code from those suggested by the Illuminating Engineering Society. This is often done by a department head, city council, or state legislature at the recommendation of an industry-dominated advisory committee or following the informal advice of local lighting interests, without public hearings or discussion. If this has occurred, it may be possible to use low-key persuasion to reduce the standards in the same way that they were raised. Normally, however, persuasion tactics will meet only indifference or open opposition from the lighting lobby.

This means that open criticism of the lighting lobby, which has representatives in every state and nearly every local community, is in order. Often employees of utility companies or fixture firms serve as unpaid advisers to help local governments set standards. The local chapter of the Illuminating Engineering Society is usually active as well. Although the IES claims to be dedicated to impartial public service, it is in reality a close ally of the lighting industry. For example, a recent speech of a former IES president in Boston was advertised in the following way:

How to sell the tremendously growing lighting market through higher IES lighting levels so that we—the engineer, manufacturer, distributor, electrical contractor, utility, and the ultimate buyer—will all benefit.

The order of beneficiaries appropriately mirrors IES's commitment to the public interest. The consumer is at the bottom.

The citizen group or lone activist working to lower standards should be prepared for a counterattack from these groups and should be ready to expose their economic interests. (A side project might be to investigate the composition of state IES members and expose their self-interest in higher lighting levels.)

This issue is an ideal one for public hearings. If the appeal is framed in terms of consumer protection, environmental preservation, and tax savings, it should receive a good response, especially if citizen groups active in these areas have been previously contacted and informed of the project. Hearings require a great deal of preparation, since the opposition will undoubtedly come armed with learned studies supported by Ph.D. testimony. However, the weight of evidence clearly supports lower standards and the tough-minded citizen who is well prepared can present a convincing case, especially when aided by allies from consumer, environmental, and tax reform groups.

In communities where no formal standards are written into law, it is more difficult to lower lighting levels. The first step is to discover what levels are ordinarily used. Local builders or architects may be willing to supply citizen investigators with some information. Blueprints on record in a public office—usually that of the town clerk or the building inspector—specify light levels. These blueprints should be matters of public information and available to all citizens. If this information is unavailable, a photographic light meter can be used, though the reading will have to be converted into foot-candles. If lighting levels above 50 foot-candles are found, they are probably too high and should be reduced. This can be done by a change in the size or number of the fixtures.

More important, the citizens group should strive to get rational standards written into law. The citizens group should bring its information to the board of education, hospital boards, building departments, and the city council to make these officials aware of the cost of too much light. The most difficult obstacle to overcome is the sacred cow of better light equaling better sight. Therefore, evidence from scientific authorities such as the ones cited in this article should be carefully marshaled and the citizens group should be prepared to rebut the arguments of IES and other vested interests.

Lowering lighting levels will not by itself solve the energy crisis. But a 50 percent slash in present levels will save $3.5 billion per year at no cost in health or efficiency. It will also significantly reduce energy consumption. A further benefit is that a campaign for rational lighting can be the opening wedge in a larger effort to increase citizen participation in vital decisions such as whether to construct more nuclear power plants, transmission line sitings, and utility rate hearings.

The following is a sample petition submitted by a Wisconsin environmental group (Wisconsin's Environmental Decade) to rationalize state lighting standards.

July 20, 1972

Industry, Labor and Human Relations Commission
310 Price Place
Madison, Wisconsin 53702

RE: Petition for repeal of a rule
under s. 227.015

Gentlemen:

Pursuant to s. 227.015, 1971 stats., Wisconsin's Environmental Decade petitions the Industry, Labor and Human Relations Commission for the repeal of a rule.

Substance or nature of the rule-making requested. Petitioner requests the repeal of Ind 19.04, Ind 19.06, Ind 19.08, Ind 19.09, Ind 19.15 and Ind 19.16, Wisconsin Administrative Code, until such time as the Commission can have a new and valid study of minimum requirements for visibility and visual comfort conducted and recommendations made for a new Illumination Code.

Reasons for the request and the petitioner's interest in the request. The sections of the Administrative Code whose repeal is requested are part of the Illumination Code. The purpose of the Illumination Code, as it is understood by the petitioner, is to provide a level of visibility and visual comfort in public buildings (as defined in Ind 19.01) that protects the public's life, health, safety and welfare. The measuring standard used to define such objective in the Illumination Code is predominantly "footcandles." Petitioner contends:

That footcandles have a dubious relation to visibility and visual comfort;

That increasing footcandles yields increasingly insignificant gains in visibility (e.g. raising footcandle levels from 3 to 18 increases the percentage of maximum visibility 12%, raising footcandle levels from 30 to 40 only increases the percentage of visibility 3%, and raising footcandle levels greater than 50 provides almost no gain in visibility at all);

That visibility and visual comfort are determined by a complex mix of variables (e.g. organization of visual facts, existence of disorganized or irrelevant visual facts, background competition, etc.), and not predominantly by footcandles;

That above minimum levels, significantly below the minimum footcandle requirements in the Illumination Code, the quantity of light is not as important as the quality;

That the footcandle requirements in the Illumination Code were established in 1964 by an advisory committee whose members had conflicts of interest which should have disqualified them from being given such rule-making authority (e.g. two of its six members were utility executives and the third was tied to them); and

That the Illuminating Engineering Society which makes the recommendations for minimum footcandle requirements nationwide, and which influenced the 1964 Wisconsin advisory committee, is in reality a merchandising utility trade association intent on selling more electricity (e.g. 14 out of 19 of its national officers are also employees of power companies, lamp manufacturers or lighting fixture companies).

Furthermore, petitioner contends that reducing needless footcandle requirements will reduce the demand for electricity. Such an action would have two desirable effects.

As the first, it would help avert an energy crisis in a manner consistent with protecting the state's natural resources.

As the second, it would make it possible for schools to use the money not spent on needless electricity to be used to purchase books and other essentials; and for offices and factories to transfer the money not spent on needless electricity to productive capacity.

Wisconsin's Environmental Decade was incorporated under ch. 181, 1969 stats., to work to protect Wisconsin's environment. As such, it has an inherent interest in reducing the growth in demand for electricity which is a paramount threat to the state's natural heritage.

References to the authority of the agency to take the action which is requested. The authority of the Commission to take such action lies in ss. 101.09 and 227.014 (2) (a), when read in conjunction with s. 1.11 (3), 1971 stats.

Thank you for your attention in this matter.

How to Establish and Run a Buyers Action Center and an Automobile Safety and Complaint Center

Each of these projects, although their specific goals differ, can be organized in essentially the same way. To avoid duplication, a brief introduction explaining the general purposes of a Buyers Action Center and an Automobile Safety and Complaint Center will be followed by a common plan describing in detail what is required to establish them.

BUYERS ACTION CENTER: AN INTRODUCTION

One way for consumers to protect themselves is to join together to form a Buyers Action Center (BAC). Buyers Action Centers can assume different forms, but each has the same basic mission—to represent consumer interests. At one extreme, a BAC may be nothing more than a loose-knit confederation interested in consumer education efforts. It may also be a tightly organized action unit with a full-time staff dedicated to protecting citizens' rights in the marketplace. Between these poles are variations on the same basic concept. The type of BAC to be formed in a particular community is a matter for local decision. Clearly, that choice will be governed by the resources, ambitions, energies, and philosophies of the initial organizers.

A BAC can perform some or all of the following services:

1. Conduct consumer education programs explaining

credit costs, unit pricing, comparative shopping techniques, etc.

2. Research and publicize advertising claims, food quality, credit policies or pricing patterns in different areas of the city.

3. Train local consumer advocates to represent citizens in disputes with manufacturers or retailers.

4. Set up a consumer complaint phone number to give individual consumers a means of securing advice or help. All complaints would be referred to appropriate government agencies or handled by the staff of the Center.

5. Develop consumer programs or public service announcements for local radio and television stations.

6. Organize picketing and other forms of last-resort protest against chronically unscrupulous merchants.

7. Help victimized consumers prepare and present their cases in small claims court.

A BAC can function as a complaint processing agency servicing individual consumer complaints, or only handle those which affect the entire community. Ideally, resources permitting, both would be pursued but different skills and personnel are required for each. If consumer education is to be emphasized, teaching and communication skills are essential. Complaint handling requires bargaining and negotiating talent. Timidity doesn't disqualify one from preparing radio or television spots, but it probably eliminates a person from leading a consumer picket. Thus, it is important to match jobs with talents. Organizers must assess as accurately as possible the various skills that they or other volunteers possess, and determine which programs they are best suited to carry out successfully.

AUTOMOBILE SAFETY AND COMPLAINT CENTER: AN INTRODUCTION

New cars reach their owners with an average of twenty-five defects, some of which may be serious. Most owners will spot some of the defects and report them to the dealer, but it is the fortunate owner indeed who succeeds in getting them corrected the first, second, or even the third time back to the shop. Even if successful, his joy may be short-lived with the appearance of additional problems which seem to come as standard equipment in a new car.

For those who cannot get their cars fixed and who are forced to take their complaint beyond the dealer level, there is little justice. Writing the manufacturer usually brings a polite letter of acknowledgment and not much more. Complaining about a dealer's refusal to fix a car still under warranty may result in a cursory check by the manufacturer's zone representative, but if he decides against the owner, no appeal is possible. Additional letters, phone calls, or telegrams will produce more form letters and, after a while, stony silence.

Manufacturers are fully aware that the rebuffed consumer has no place to turn. Despite advertising claims to the contrary, consumers have no choice but to accept cars that are poorly designed, badly assembled, and built to undergo varying degrees of self-destruction while still relatively new. In the aggregate, this amounts annually to a multibillion-dollar fraud. In effect, the owner pays for the manufacturer's mistakes and sloppiness.

At present the three major avenues for redress—through the manufacturer, the courts, or administrative agencies—are inaccessible to the consumer stuck with a lemon. Manufacturers and retailers are generally unwilling to do much, especially if the complaint involves a major claim. The

courts are effectively closed to all but the largest cases of
consumer fraud. If injury or death is involved, the courts
are useful because settlement may result in very high
damages. In smaller cases not involving personal injury, the
costs of litigation, especially attorney's fees, are so prohibi-
tively expensive that often it is cheaper to pay for repairs
or buy a new product than to take a case to court.

In some areas, small claims court (see page 205) offers
citizens a valuable alternative to the traditional court system. Its chief advantage is that citizens can present their
own cases without incurring expensive court costs or having
to pay attorney's fees. Procedures are relaxed to allow the
case to be argued informally. These courts could be very
useful, although overcrowding and scheduling problems,
which sometimes result in long postponements, can often
discourage citizens from pursuing their rights.

The last avenue available to the consumer is through the
administrative procedures of government. But most communities don't have consumer agencies set up to help individual consumers through the administrative maze. Lacking
the financial resources to use the courts and without access
to government agencies, consumers must seek new ways to
protect their rights.

Buyers Action Centers and Automobile Safety and Research Centers are proven methods for helping individual
citizens deal with consumer problems. There already are
five operating automobile centers and many more consumer
centers. A few scattered centers, of course, don't have the
power to instigate fundamental reforms of the buyer-seller
relationship. What is needed is a nationwide network of
cooperating centers whose combined strength might well
be sufficient to bring these about.

The Consumer Federation of America (CFA), 1012 14th
Street, N.W., Washington, D.C. 20005, has chapters in
many parts of the country. Some are effective advocates of
consumer welfare; others are passive. Before setting out to
start a new center, it is worth checking the local CFA
branch to learn what it is doing. At the very least, new

allies may be found. At best, the citizens group might be able to interest CFA in starting the center itself. In addition to CFA, there are other citizen groups who might be able to offer assistance. Before starting an Auto Complaint Center, contact the Center for Auto Safety, P.O. Box 7250, Ben Franklin Station, Washington, D.C. 20044.

HOW TO START A CENTER

Establishing a center is not a casual enterprise to be undertaken lightly. Operating a successful center requires stamina, courage, diplomacy, toughness, and a certain amount of administrative talent. It also requires funds to cover such unavoidable expenses as phones, mail, and travel. Finally, a core staff of one or two permanent and several part-time volunteers are needed to run the center effectively. Permanent volunteers are especially important because it is they who will provide expertise and continuity, and it is they who will, to a large extent, set the tone for the operation.

The first step when considering opening a center is to gather background materials on basic consumer problems and methods for dealing with them. All of the organizers should have a general familiarity with the more common problems. The following books are good background reading on consumer problems:

Council for the Deceived by Philip Shrag (Pantheon Books, 1972).

The Poor Pay More by David Caplovitz (The Free Press of Glencoe, 1963).

Hot War on the Consumer by David Sanford (Pittman Publishing Company, 1970).

The Dark Side of the Marketplace by Senator Warren Magnuson and Jean Carper (Prentice-Hall, 1968).

One of the best sources of information on tactics to protect consumers CEPA, the Consumer Education and Protection Association, 6048 Ogontz Avenue, Philadelphia, Pennsylvania 19141. A copy of the history of CEPA can be obtained from them for three dollars. If an Automobile Center is planned, *What to Do with Your Bad Car* by Ralph Nader, Lowell Dodge, and Ralph Hotchkiss (Grossman, 1971), *Unsafe at Any Speed* by Ralph Nader (expanded and updated edition, Grossman, 1972) and *Small—On Safety: The Designed-in Dangers of the Volkswagen,* by the Center for Auto Safety (Grossman, 1972) are good introductions to automotive safety issues.

Step two is to locate at least two or three volunteers willing to work almost full-time at the center for the first six months of its operation; one of these should be tentatively committed to remaining with the center beyond the initial stage. In addition to this core of semi-permanent volunteers, other part-time volunteers should be recruited. As a general rule, no center should open without a two-person core staff and five to ten part-time volunteers. An effort should be made to find at least one mechanic sympathetic to the aims of the center and willing to offer advice.

Housewives are an excellent source of personnel who have the time, energy, and interest to staff consumer or automobile centers, since many of them have skills which are underutilized. They are also familiar with community affairs and because of their purchasing power can exert considerable pressure on local merchants.

Another way to staff the center is to organize it as a special project of an existing organization. Service clubs, consumer groups, socially active church committees, and other similar citizen organizations might prove very receptive to the idea. Such groups provide built-in constituency support, as well as a ready source of volunteers. Another good source of volunteers is the student community. At some schools, such as the University of Maryland and Kansas State, student governments have undertaken to sponsor consumer centers to serve the university community, and have subsequently expanded to aid the entire community.

Enough funds must be on hand to start the center and to keep it going. If only local complaints are handled and office supplies are used sparingly, the center should be able to operate on less than $100 a month, excluding rent. Because there will be some initial start-up costs (phone deposits, purchase of supplies, and the like) it is best to have raised or have strong prospects of raising $1,000 during the first six months. Less might be required, but it is better to be on the safe side.

To house the center, a volunteer's garage, a room in a church basement, an office in a student activities building, or any other available free space can be used. If the center is not going to handle walk-in complaints, the office does not have to be easily accessible to the general public. If walk-in complaints are going to be encouraged, a storefront office is probably best. The only equipment needed is a phone with two or three numbers and as many extensions, a few tables and chairs, a filing cabinet, a typewriter, and a small quantity of basic office supplies.

It is important to obtain the *pro bono* (free) services of a lawyer to prepare articles of incorporation and to file for nonprofit, tax exempt status under 26 U.S. Code Section 501(c)(3). It is best to incorporate the center because this limits the staff's liability; moreover, donations to a nonprofit, tax exempt center are tax deductible. However, in some areas of the country it takes six to nine months to get the Internal Revenue Service to approve a 501(c)(3) status, so it is not wise to count on raising initial money with the lure of a tax deduction.

After these preliminary steps are successfully completed, the core staff should begin to train thoroughly for the job ahead. The techniques of negotiating cannot be learned from books, though they can be developed by simulated problem handling and role playing. The best way to learn is by doing. After the center is operating, new volunteers can learn by apprenticing themselves to more experienced workers. It usually doesn't take long for a novice to be turned into a hard-nosed "professional."

Channels of communication with local media and other consumer and environmental organizations should be opened. Public pressure is the strongest force available to the center and the better the access to the media and the more allies committed to the center's goals, the more likely will be its eventual success.

Initially, however, the center should spread news of its existence slowly. A major press release heralding the answer to consumers' prayers will bring an unmanageable deluge of complaints. Techniques should be well-honed on a few cases before a major effort to gain public awareness is undertaken.

HOW TO OPERATE A CENTER

Ordinarily, the following day-to-day operating procedure should be observed:

First, every complaint that cannot be disposed of in the initial phone call should be "registered" by the volunteer phone answerer. Registration involves taking down basic information about the complainant—name, address, phone number, a concise statement of the grievance, and, in the case of an auto center, year and make of car and dealer. In the case of an appliance or other consumer item, the store and the type of purchase should be recorded along with the nature of the problem.

Second, a volunteer trained in follow-up techniques should recontact the complainant and investigate carefully the validity of the grievance. Not every charge of manufacturer or dealer perfidy is true, and to maintain its credibility the center must make every effort to strain out frivolous complaints. The caseworker must also make sure that the person complaining is willing to follow through on the complaint and not back down at the first sign of manufacturer or dealer resistance. For this reason, it is well to get a signed statement from the complainant authorizing the center to act in his behalf.

Third, the manufacturer or dealer should be contacted to attempt to work out an amicable settlement in favor of the consumer. Often a careful reading of the warranty in the case of new car or certain appliances will disclose the fact that the consumer has an absolute right to the repair or replacement requested. Even if specific coverage is not provided, dealers often will make a swift settlement rather than bother with a protracted customer dispute. This kind of response should be increasingly frequent as the center gains a reputation in the community.

If negotiations reach a stalemate, some form of affirmative action must be taken. There are various tactics available to lemon owners—from consumer picketing, to parking the car in front of the dealer's showroom with a large lemon sign and an explanation of what is wrong, to obtaining unfavorable media coverage for the particular dealer. "The Living History of CEPA" and CEPA's regular newsletter provide information about strategies applicable in other situations where consumers have been abused. Different circumstances require different tactics, but as a rule the center should pursue a gradually escalating series of actions to avoid getting locked into an intransigent position without maneuvering room or further reserves.

In addition to handling basic complaints, there are other services which an Automobile Safety and Complaint Center can perform. If a cooperative automobile mechanic can be found, the center can begin a course in elementary automobile repair. Courses being offered now by some centers are divided into beginning and advanced sessions, each consisting of five two-hour lessons for a nominal charge of three dollars per lesson. If the teacher's services are donated, several classes of five or ten people per week can provide enough money to sustain the other activities of the center. More information on repair courses can be obtained by writing Mr. Pat Goss, 5301 Kenilworth Avenue, Riverdale, Maryland 20040.

Similar programs can be instituted by imaginative organizers of a Buyers Action Center. The center could offer lecturers or instruction in technical subjects such as what to look for when purchasing a new car or a new home, or how to evaluate insurance policies or pension plans. The center can form a speakers bureau to provide speakers to schools or to local community groups. If groups can afford it, small donations to the center can be requested for the speaker's services. A special task force can prepare weekly radio spots giving information about particular products or warning consumers about different consumer frauds. This information should also be placed in local newspapers, club newsletters, or even church bulletins.

Centers can join forces on specific issues to increase their impact. Existing automobile centers are already feeding data to the vehicle defect division of the Department of Transportation with the aim of spotting design defects at an earlier stage in a car's life.

Finally, consumer centers can form the nucleus of a larger citizens' lobbying effort. Through phone contacts and letters the center should build up a list of area residents concerned with consumer problems in a relatively short time. These contacts can be welded into a lobby to push for reform at the town, county, and state levels. Don't forget that your goal is not just to resolve complaints but to see that businesses do not repeat their offenses.

II

SOME PRESCRIPTIONS FOR BETTER HEALTH CARE

Every day, over three million Americans seek medical care, some for sickness, for injury, for serious problems and for minor ones. For almost all the attempt to find adequate care is likely to be frustrating. The United States has far too few doctors and its huge investment in medical care facilities has not always been spent wisely. Consequently, many people, especially the poor, find it difficult to obtain decent medical treatment. The effects of these problems can be seen in health statistics. Despite its number-one economic ranking, the United States finishes back in the pack when it comes to health care. Each year at least thirty-three thousand babies die unnecessarily before their first birthdays. Fifty thousand workers are killed and as many as twenty-five million are injured on the job. An American male's life expectancy ranks below that of men in seventeen other nations.

Economic statistics are also revealing. Americans pay more for health care than citizens in any other nation. The costs of health-related services are equally high. Prescrip-

tion drug costs consistently rise. Hospital costs have risen
so far so fast that hospital care is priced beyond the reach of
most of the more than twenty million Americans not covered by health insurance. Rising health insurance costs
strain the resources of millions of other citizens.

The projects in this section touch on many important
areas of medical care. All of them aim to increase the
amount of citizen representation in the health area. It is
only through greater citizen participation that the nation's
medical philosophy can be rationalized so that human
needs take precedence over profits or doctor convenience.
When that philosophy is made rational, and when citizens
are made active and enlightened participants in the provision of medical services, the grim statistics of disease and
its cost may begin to change.

How to Lower the Price
of Prescription Drugs*

A recent study by the Federal Trade Commission showed
that the pharmaceutical industry is one of the most profit-
able in the United States. This is not a new phenomenon
nor is it surprising. Americans spend over five billion
annually for prescription drugs alone. Additional billions
are spent for over-the-counter drugs that don't require
prescriptions. The people who spend the most are often
those who can afford it the least—the old, the infirm, and
the parents of young children.

What accounts for the high cost of prescription drugs?

* A more complete version of this project, entitled "An Outline
for Consumer Action on Prescription Drugs," is available in
limited quantities from the Health Research Group, 2000 P
Street, N.W., Washington, D.C. 20036. Free.

Certainly research and especially development of products which differ from existing ones only enough to win a patent for the developer contribute to the overhead expense. But more important is the fact that doctors are bombarded with "detail men" (drug salesmen) and promotional materials for specific drug products. The drug industry annually spends $600 million to $800 million on a massive promotion campaign aimed at physicians. Using paid advertisements in medical journals, endless free samples, and large sales forces, *the pharmaceutical companies spend three to four thousand dollars in promotion for every physician practicing in the United States.* The cost of this promotional effort is roughly twenty-five cents of every drug sales dollar. Theoretically, if promotion expenses alone were eliminated, Americans could save $1.25 billion a year. The situation is compounded by antisubstitution laws which prohibit a pharmacist from substituting a cheaper, less-advertised brand in place of the specific brand written on the prescription. For example, a recent survey in Washington, D.C., showed one brand of 100 250-mg. tablets of tetracycline (a common antibiotic) selling for $1.40 and another brand of 100 tablets selling for $6.00. There is no difference between the two brands—except the name and the price.

The sole reason that a bottle of 100 250-mg. tablets of tetracycline costs $1.40 while another costs over four times as much is that one is the generic drug and the other a brand name. *Generic* refers to all drugs with the same active components. There will be a single generic name, such as penicillin, for a drug which is sold under several brand names. *Brand name* refers to the catchy title given to a drug product by the manufacturer, such as Pentids or V-Cillin-K. The brand name is designed to stick in the physician's memory and inspire him to prescribe the drug. Brand name drugs are the major kind advertised in medical journals and by detail men. Of the more than 22,000 drug products on the market, only about 1,200 represent different drug entities. The remainder are accounted for by mixtures of chemical agents with similar drug action, different dosage forms, colors, bottle sizes, and package types.

When a physician writes a prescription specifying a brand name drug it usually costs the consumer extra money. In all but two states, pharmacists are forbidden by law to dispense any drug other than the exact drug prescribed by the physician. Many states have anti-drug-substitution laws dating from the turn of the century. Their original purpose was to prevent pharmacists from dispensing products which were completely different from those called for. These laws clearly served a valuable purpose.

After World War II, the major drug manufacturers lobbied vigorously for new laws, or new interpretations of the old laws. Whereas before, druggists had been prevented from giving out a different *product* than that prescribed by the doctor, the new laws even prevented the druggist from giving out a different *brand* of the same product. The drug manufacturers argued that the changes were needed to eliminate inferior quality products—presumably made by fly-by-night manufacturers—from the market. The states bought the argument. Clearly, however, major pharmaceutical companies knew that they stood to reap huge profits by the new laws. If they had been interested only in quality, a better solution would have been more stringent government monitoring of the manufacturing process. Today, the Food and Drug Administration does just that, so that both generic and brand drugs must meet the same standards. Thus there is no longer any reason for anti-substitution laws. The only reason these laws remain on the books is that they line the pockets of drug manufacturers who are the *only* group that profits from the substitution ban.

Many pharmacists oppose these laws because they reduce their status from licensed skilled professionals, who in most cases know more about drugs than do doctors, to order takers with no more responsibility than soda jerks or sales clerks. Pharmacists have economic reasons for their opposition; if substitution were permitted they could greatly reduce their present inventories of duplicate brand name drugs.

Maryland and Kentucky recently modified their antisubstitution laws to allow some degree of substitution by pharmacists within certain guidelines. These laws are reasonable first steps, but a better law would allow pharmacists to substitute freely unless drug inequivalency were proven. Copies of a model substitution statute are available from the Health Research Group, 2000 P Street, N.W., Washington, D.C. 20036.

There is one more factor that allows brand name drug manufacturers to charge high prices: little of the advertising aimed at doctors contains price information, and prescription drugs are not usually advertised to the general public—with or without price information. Approximately thirty-eight states have statutes prohibiting price advertising of prescription drugs. Some, like Virginia, even prohibit the use of words like "discount." These laws are particularly unfair because prices for a given drug product, whether generic or brand name, may also vary widely from pharmacy to pharmacy. Once the doctor has written a brand name prescription, the consumer in most cases has no choice but to pay whatever is being charged for the product by his local pharmacy. Even comparison shopping is difficult; many pharmacists will not give prices over the telephone. How many people, sick and needing drugs immediately, can shop around from store to store? The poor, the disabled, and the old are especially limited. The direct effect of these two laws—antisubstitution and antiadvertising—is to eliminate price competition from the prescription drug industry.

Consumer efforts to combat these laws are complicated by the fact that they tend to reinforce one another. Although many pharmacists oppose antisubstitution laws, most, especially small independent pharmacists, support laws prohibiting posting of prices. Manufacturers, generally, are less concerned about posting laws. To lower the cost of prescription drugs, it is necessary to attack both laws, even though such a campaign throws pharmacists and manufacturers together into an unholy alliance. One victory without the other is not sufficient because repeal of the antisubstitution ban without a posting requirement in effect allows the pharmacist to inflate prices at his own discretion while a posting law without free substitution still leaves the consumer at the mercy of the prescription writer.

The Western Massachusetts Public Interest Research Group (WMPIRG) has recently been involved in an attempt to repeal the antisubstitution law and to institute a statewide posting law. (The city of Boston has a posting law which requires pharmacies to post on their premises the prices of 100 standard drugs. However, because enforcement is weak, compliance varies.) They began their efforts by conducting a survey of ninety drug stores, asking for price quotes for a common antibiotic, Erithromycin. Quotes ranged from $2.00 to $9.97, and the survey quickly became headline news. WMPIRG called for local posting regulations.

In Northhampton, the editor of the *Hampshire Daily Gazette*, which gave extensive coverage to the WMPIRG report, was visited by a delegation of pharmacists who demanded that the paper print their side of the story. Posting is unethical, they said, and furthermore, it would force pharmacists to be competitive. If that happened, they warned, they would be forced to buy the cheaper generic drugs. The pharmacists implied that generics were less safe, and that no doctor in the area would support generic prescribing. A reporter at the *Gazette* took the initiative, called a dozen doctors, and to the chagrin of the pharmacists nearly two-thirds supported the idea of generic prescribing.

Several things have happened since publication of the WMPIRG study. Massachusetts state public health officials are working on a generic substitution law, confident of public support. A state representative and a state senator are drafting a posting law to be introduced during the next legislative session.

The Texas Public Interest Research Group (TexPIRG) studied pharmacies in Houston and uncovered data that support WMPIRG'S findings. The same amount of the same type of penicillin, for example, varied from $0.88 to $8.00 in different pharmacies. TexPIRG researchers could find no correlation between the price of drugs and store location, amount of customer and professional services, or any other factor. Generics were consistently cheaper than brand-name drugs, but within each category prices of each drug varied widely from store to store. Copies of the TexPIRG study are available for $0.50 from TexPIRG, Box 7047, Austin, Texas.

Efforts similar to those of WMPIRG and TexPIRG can work in other states as well. The first step is to study the antisubstitution or antiadvertising provisions of state law. Usually they are included among the general laws dealing with the practice of pharmacy, but they might be found in the regulations set by the Boards of Pharmacy. Once the law is identified and its legislative history learned, the next step is to demonstrate that the law serves no valad purpose.

Natural allies in a fight to pass posting laws and to permit free substitution of generic drugs are consumer groups, organizations of retired people (people over sixty-five account for only 10 percent of the population, but 25 percent of prescription drug sales), state and local chapters of the League of Women Voters, the American Association of University Women, welfare rights groups or other organizations representing the poor, labor unions, and some local political party groups. The American Pharmaceutical Association (APhA), representing 38,000 pharmacists and 13,000 pharmacy students, is a strong supporter of repeal and some pharmacists and pharmacy associations affiliated with it can probably be counted on to lend assistance against antisubstitution laws. Large, high-volume pharmacists may also favor posting laws.

Opposition will come primarily from brand name drug

manufacturers, and from some conservative medical associations who fear that allowing a pharmacist to change a brand name to a generic name will take away the doctor's "prerogative" as the sole practitioner of medicine. This fear is groundless, since no one has shown more than a few generic and brand name drugs to be different. Its roots lie less in concern for possible harm to the patient than in nervousness about demythologizing the practice of medicine. The opponents of repeal or modification are well-financed, well-organized, and prepared to fight hard to protect their multimillion-dollar golden goose.

Step three is to build broad public support for a generic substitution law. Data on the annual cost of antisubstitution laws to consumers can be collected and presented to the media and the public in appropriately dramatic ways. A list of the most common prescription drugs comparing the cost of generic and brand names can be prepared and released to the media or presented at citizen hearings (see page 179). Expert witnesses can present facts to show that most opposition is motivated by self-interest alone. Other witnesses can dispel fears of inferior-quality products if substitution is permitted. Finally, the issue must be presented as a *consumer* matter, for it is not a medical question. Politicians should be forced to choose sides on this consideration alone. The same steps can be taken to build support for a posting law. A survey similar to WMPIRG's can greatly aid this effort.

Step four is to persuade sympathetic legislators to introduce bills repealing the antisubstitution law and requiring posting of prescription drug prices. Especially in an election year, politicians should be able to overcome pharmaceutical industry pressure in exchange for support at the polls from grateful consumers. The final step in the process is to build up overwhelming consumer pressure to lobby for passage of a strong bill (see page 174 for hints on lobbying techniques). If a broad-based coalition has been built, this last step should be easier.

Even if the effort to repeal antisubstitution legislation

proves unsuccessful, there are steps that the individual consumer can take to save money. These, however, are relatively weak compared to the benefits that would flow from passage of a substitution statute.

HINTS ON HOW TO SAVE MONEY WHEN USING PRESCRIPTION DRUGS

—Ask your physician to prescribe only generic drugs. If he refuses, ask him why *he* prefers brand names, even though they cost *you* more. Consider switching to another physician if his answer is unsatisfactory.

—Ask your pharmacist whether he favors substitution. If he does, enlist his support in repealing antisubstitution laws. If he opposes it, find out why. Point out that generic substitution will permit him to stock larger quantities of fewer items and thus save money by avoiding a large inventory.

—Do comparison shopping. Assuming you read the often illegible prescription (if you cannot, ask the doctor to rewrite it legibly), phone or visit several pharmacies and ask the pharmacist the price of the prescription. Even between different brand names there may be substantial price differences.

—Keep records of the drugs you take and what they cost. If prices of the same drug vary significantly over a short period of time, ask your pharmacist why. Compare these prices with other pharmacies.

An important fact to remember is that medicine is a consumer purchase and bargains should be hunted as zealously where drugs are concerned as they are with any other product that has to adhere to uniform quality standards.

How to Do a Toy Safety Survey

> Hundreds of thousands of children are needlessly injured, and many killed, each year in the United States. These children are wounded and maimed and put to death, not by sex fiends, or invading armies or maniacal and sadistic parents or ravaging diseases; they are the victims of their own playthings.
>
> —Edward M. Swartz, *Toys That Don't Care*

People normally associate toys with the joys of childhood. But many people associate toys with children burned, lacerated, blinded, disfigured, or killed. The U.S. Public Health Service estimates that more than 700,000 children are injured annually in toy-related accidents. Swings hurt another 500,000 and slides 200,000 more. Most of these injuries are minor, but an alarming number are serious. Many could be prevented or diminished in severity by safer, better-designed toys.

The Child Protection and Toy Safety Act of 1969, which is an amendment to the Hazardous Substances Act, is the major piece of federal legislation relating to toys. The act empowers the Department of Health, Education, and Welfare (HEW) to promulgate regulations banning from sale in interstate commerce any "toy or other article intended for use by children" if it "presents an electrical, mechanical, or thermal hazard" by causing "an unreasonable risk of personal injury or illness." The test for whether a toy presents a thermal hazard, for example, is whether "in normal use or when subjected to reasonably foreseeable damage or abuse, its design or manufacture presents an unreasonable risk of personal injury or illness because of heat as from heated parts, substances, or surfaces."

Unfortunately it took the Food and Drug Administration

(FDA) until November, 1971, two years after the passage of the act, to publish the regulations on mechanical hazards; regulations on thermal and electrical hazards will not be completed until "sometime in 1973," according to FDA.

While the act is deficient in several respects (for example, it does not provide for mandatory standards of safety for toys), it nevertheless gives the FDA considerable power. If the Secretary of HEW finds that the toy or article presents an *imminent hazard* to the public, it can ban the article from sale pending the completion of administrative proceedings. However, the Secretary of HEW has not used this power. FDA can take a manufacturer to court (but had not done so through 1972) and can seize products in interstate commerce (sixteen seizures were made in fiscal year 1972). Altogether, it is a dismal record given the magnitude and seriousness of the problem.

In 1973, the new Consumer Product Safety Commission will take over the administration of the federal Hazardous Substances Act and the Flammable Fabrics Act, both of which cover children's products. This independent regulatory commission will assume many of the responsibilities formerly exercised by FDA's Bureau of Product Safety.

Consumers will have to keep the pressure on in the area of children's hazards to ensure that the new commission is not sluggish. Toy surveys conducted by consumer groups in Arkansas, Minnesota, Ohio, and Washington, and a large effort by public interest groups during the 1972 holiday season, revealed that many of the 900 toys banned by FDA were still on the shelves and that other toys, having the same defects as those banned, continue to be marketed without government interference. More than 90 percent of the toys tested by the Minnesota Public Interest Research Group (MPIRG) in April, 1972, and found to be hazardous, are not at present banned by FDA and can be sold freely.

This lack of enforcement leaves the individual consumer with little protection. Even the most recent FDA action setting up citizens' committees on toy safety (Consumer

Deputy Pilot Program) is a partial measure at best, and indications are that it is more an attempt to silence critics than to solve the toy safety problem. The citizens' committees have very little power. Consumer deputies cannot open packages, cannot describe themselves as FDA employees, and even are forbidden to use publicity. All reports must be sent directly to FDA. They are supposed to survey twenty-five retail outlets a month and give managers the current banned toy list, but are to do nothing else regardless of what abuses they find.

A toy survey is not child's play. It requires both perseverance and meticulous thoroughness since, unlike prices or labels, which are obvious, identifying banned or unsafe toys with hidden hazards requires a certain degree of skill. The results of the survey must be widely disseminated so that it has an impact on retailers and influences consumer buying decisions. Timeliness is a critical factor. Conducting a survey in January is not very useful, since most toy purchases are made in the six weeks before Christmas. For maximum effect, the survey should be conducted during October and released to the public in early to mid-November. An active group of surveyors can continue to generate attention throughout the holiday season with additional publicity releases identifying particularly unsafe toys, or by affirmative action against the retailer who refuses to remove banned toys from his shelves. This action might involve appeals to the new commission to seize the toys, warnings in churches or in leaflets distributed in front of the offending retail establishment, or the use of public service radio and television spots for counter-commercials.

ORGANIZING A SURVEY

The first step in conducting a toy safety survey is to gather background information. *Toys That Don't Care* by Edward M. Swartz (Gambit, 1971) is excellent background preparation; it will help explain the features to look for in unsafe toys. A copy of the Minnesota Public Interest Research Group's survey can be obtained free by writing MPIRG, 3036 University Avenue, S.E., Minneapolis, Minnesota 55414. The District of Columbia Public Interest Research Group's evaluation of the FDA's toy safety efforts is available for $0.50 from D.C. PIRG, 800 21st Street N.W., Room 435, Washington, D.C. 20036. A copy of the 1969 Child Protection and Toy Safety Act, along with other relevant legislation, the list of banned toys, and all applicable regulations can be obtained from the Consumer Product Safety Commission.

The team of surveyors must be familiar with the problems of toy safety and prepared to devote considerable time and energy over a period of several weeks. The Minnesota survey encompassed forty-one stores in the Minneapolis–St. Paul area and required three surveyors working several hours a day for a period of three weeks. Most other groups have used ten to fifteen volunteers, thus considerably shortening the survey time.

The survey itself should start with the largest stores and work down to smaller, less frequented stores. This way, if time runs out or surveyors begin to tire, at least the most important stores will have been covered.

When the survey is completed, its release should be aimed at attracting the widest possible attention from the media, especially if it is conducted just before the Hanukkah and Christmas buying season. One articulate person should be appointed to make a presentation of survey findings at a press conference. If funds permit, the surveyors should display several samples of unsafe toys. Nothing is more properly dramatic, especially for television consumption, than an actual demonstration of a safety hazard, such as showing how hot toy ovens become, the inflammability of a fabric, or the ease with which a rubber tip is removed from a toy dart, leaving a sharp wooden or plastic point. Each reporter at the conference should be supplied with a copy of the survey's findings and, if a follow-up is planned, a phone number where anxious consumers can call for information. But be warned that the number of calls is likely to overwhelm normal facilities and special arrangements should be made.

The survey results should also be presented to store managers with a demand that hazardous toys be removed from the shelves at once and that customers who have unwittingly purchased unsafe toys be permitted to return them and receive a complete refund. If the store is part of a chain, a letter signed by as many customers as can be found should be sent to its president with a copy of the results and a request that he immediately order harmful toys removed from all branch stores. Copies of the letter should be sent to the Consumer Product Safety Commission, local congressmen and state legislators, the state attorney general, local consumer agencies, and Consumers Union (1714 Massachusetts Avenue, Washington, D.C. 20036).

To keep up the pressure and the publicity, gather signatures on a petition calling for the elimination of hazardous toys from store shelves. To give the petition added impact, signatures should be solicited from school children who, while young, are certainly capable of understanding the dangers of hazardous toys. They purchase one-third of the toys sold annually, so they can protest both as the consumers and the victims of toys.

Groups serious about eliminating children's hazards should be familiar with the current regulations or the gaps in the regulations concerning bicycles, playground equipment, infant furniture, inflammable pajamas, and so forth, all of which are under the supervision of the new commission and thus a logical extension of a toy safety survey.

A repurchase campaign is another way to keep pressure on manufacturers and to force them to pretest articles. The 1969 law requires all sellers of banned hazardous substances to repurchase such substances from the buyers of them, in accordance with regulations of the Secretary of HEW. The Secretary, however, neglected to formulate the regulations and eventually Ralph Nader filed suit to compel him to do so in September, 1972. On December 19, 1972, the FDA proposed regulations governing repurchase, but at time of publication of this book, they have not become final.

Groups which have already formed a working coalition to survey stores can use their organization to encourage parents who purchased banned children's articles to return these to the retailers. Bad publicity, accompanied by a decline in the seller's profits, will force both retailer and manufacturer to take important preventive measures. If the group desires, it can urge buyers to shop at those stores stocking only pretested toys and flame-retardant materials.

Child safety is an issue capable of arousing strong community reaction. A citizen effort focusing attention on toy safety may stimulate a city government to examine more closely other issues which have profound effects on child health, such as poison control, drug packaging, and school bus safety. State laws can be strengthened and federal agencies in turn can be pressured to do more than sponsor public education campaigns which often shift an unfair burden of responsibility back to the consumer.

At the very least, a well-done toy safety survey will not only protect children but also enlist the respect and support of numerous community groups. If a group of citizens is interested in establishing an on-going consumer movement or a Buyers Action Center (see page 59), a toy safety survey and a repurchase campaign can provide excellent launching pads for future action.

How to Enforce the Occupational Safety and Health Act for Yourself and for Others

Each year over fourteen thousand American workers are killed on the job, and estimates of the number injured range from two million to twenty-five million. The number who die from occupational illnesses is even more grim—a hundred thousand a year die according to 1972 estimates of the National Institute of Occupational Safety and Health. This shocking figure makes occupation-related death, disease, and disability the leading forms of violence in the United States.

Workers' lives are constantly threatened by coal dust, cotton dust, asbestos, lead, benzene, mercury, and thousands of other toxic substances. The deadly cumulative effects of many of these substances often do not show up until years after initial exposure. The coal miner, for example, doesn't contract black lung with his first deep breath in a dust-filled mine. Nor does the truck driver lose his hearing the instant the noise level in the cab of his truck soars 30 or 40 decibels above the legal limit. But both are being slowly and insidiously injured by their day-to-day contact with these hazards. As a result, thousands of workers suffer from occupational diseases like black lung, brown lung, emphysema, cancer of the bladder, asbestosis, and noise-induced hearing loss. The grim toll of these diseases is documented in *Bitter Wages: Ralph Nader's Study Group Report on Disease and Injury on the Job,* by Joseph A. Page and Mary-Win O'Brien (Grossman, 1973).

Until recently there was no way for a worker facing an

occupational hazard to protect himself legally. Then in 1970, after many delaying actions, Congress passed the Occupational Safety and Health Act. The law gives the Secretary of Labor the power to set standards for harmful chemical and physical agents in the workplace; requires employers to keep records about safety and health conditions in their plants and to issue citations for violations; and, most important, permits workers to take independent action to protect themselves.

This last provision is important because the law and its administration contain serious defects. The standards in many cases are unacceptable and don't cover thousands of toxic substances found in the workplace. The penalty provisions are inadequate (last year's average penalty proposed for a violation was twenty-five dollars) and the appeals procedure is a long and complicated one. The power of the Secretary of Labor is in some ways too restricted. These are built-in weaknesses but, although serious, they are not so dangerous to the worker as the lack of adequate enforcement.

A good law can be undermined by nonexistent or haphazard enforcement just as a bad law can be strengthened by vigorous enforcement. Unfortunately, the Occupational Safety and Health Act is an example of a mediocre law dangerously weakened by lax enforcement. The law was designed "to assure as far as possible every working man and woman in the nation safe and healthful working conditions." It applies to an estimated 57 million workers and 4.1 million workplaces in the United States. Workplaces with one employee are currently covered as well as those with 5,000 employees, although there have been recent efforts to undermine the act further by exempting small businesses from coverage. And "workplace" is interpreted to include, among others, construction sites, factories, farms, ranches, cabs of trucks, and any other "area, workplace or environment where work is being performed."

But to carry out this immense responsibility there are only some 375 actual inspectors in the entire United States,

75 of whom are assigned to maritime inspections. The remaining 300 are divided about evenly into (1) inspections of five specific "target industries" and "target health hazards," (2) investigations of fatalities and employee complaints, and (3) random investigations of workplaces. The target industries are marine cargo handling, roofing and sheet metal work, meat processing, lumber, and transportation equipment. Target health hazards include asbestos, cotton dust, silica, lead, and carbon monoxide. With so limited a number of inspectors, any other hazardous workplace obviously has little chance of being inspected unless a worker files a complaint with the Department of Labor.

For these reasons the employee cannot sit back and relax, confident that he or she is protected by the Occupational Safety and Health Act. Employees must vigorously assert the rights guaranteed them by the act to ensure their own protection. There is much that the employee can do to improve the quality of the workplace.

To begin with, know what your rights are. The act requires every employer to display a poster titled Safety and Health Protection on the Job. The poster briefly explains employee rights under the law. If it isn't displayed, the employer is violating the law and can be fined and required to put it up. To become more familiar with employee rights guaranteed by the act, additional information is easily obtainable. The Department of Labor (Occupational Safety and Health Administration, 14th and Constitution Avenue, N.W., Washington, D.C. 20210), the AFL-CIO (Standing Committee on Safety and Occupational Health, Room 504, 815 16th Street, N.W., Washington, D.C. 20006), and various unions have published pamphlets describing the act and workers' rights under it. An especially helpful booklet on employee rights is *Job, Health Safety and You*, published by the International Brotherhood of Teamsters (25 Louisiana Avenue, N.W., Washington, D.C. 20001). The Industrial Health and Safety Project of Urban Planning Aid (639 Massachusetts Avenue, Cambridge, Massachusetts 02139) has also published the following pamphlets:

"A Unionist's Guide to the Occupational Safety and Health Act of 1970"
"How to Inspect Your Work Place"
"A Resource List for Health and Safety Problems"
"Noise and Your Job"

Once acquainted with the general provisions of the act, an employee should be prepared to exercise his rights wherever a hazardous condition exists. If, for example, an employee wants to determine whether a substance in his workplace is dangerous, he can contact the National Institute of Occupational Safety and Health (5600 Fishers Lane, Rockville, Maryland 20852), which can send an investigator to the workplace. The Health Research Group, under the direction of Ralph Nader and Dr. Sidney Wolfe (2000 P Street, N.W., Washington, D.C. 20036), is also able to advise workers on toxic chemicals and other hazardous conditions in their workplaces. Another group actively involved in helping workers obtain safer, healthier work environments is the Medical Committee for Human Rights (710 South Marshfield, Chicago, Illinois 60612). MCHR has sponsored conferences in conjunction with local unions at which the health hazards in specific workplaces were presented to workers. Printed information on such hazards is available upon request.

Fortunately, the employee does not have to wait for a routine inspection to be made if he believes his workplace is violating standards or contains hazardous conditions. *Every employee has the right to request a federal inspection* and to do so free from fear of employer harassment. If an employer takes action against an employee because of a request for a safety and health inspection, the employee should file a complaint with the Secretary of Labor within thirty days of the action. The Secretary must investigate the situation and, if the employer has discharged the employee or discriminated against him, the Secretary must bring suit in federal court for all necessary relief including reinstatement and back pay.

THREE HAZARDOUS SITUATIONS COVERED BY INSPECTIONS

First, if a specific safety or health standard has been violated, an employee should file a written complaint with the Department of Labor specifying the violation. Employees should use a Department of Labor complaint form if one is available; otherwise, employees can write a letter to the regional administrator of the Department of Labor. (Model complaint letters are offered at the end of this section.) Complaints must be in writing and the company will receive a copy at the time of the inspection. An employee can specify that his or her name be removed from the complaint before it is given to the company. The Occupational Safety and Health Administration (OSHA) does *not* have to make an inspection if there are no reasonable grounds for believing that a violation exists. In such a case, however, it must send a written explanation to the employee.

The second hazardous situation is an "imminent danger" that might reasonably be expected to cause injury or death. If a worker complains that an imminent danger exists, OSHA *must* send an inspector to investigate. If such a danger is found to exist, the Secretary of Labor can then go into federal court and ask for an order to correct the hazard immediately.

The third hazardous situation arises where there is no specific standard and no imminent danger. Under the act, the employer has a general duty to keep the workplace free from "recognized hazards." If an employee believes a hazard exists, he or she should file a written complaint with OSHA and request an inspection.

Federal inspections, according to the law, must be undertaken with *no advance notice* to the employer except in unusual cases. In addition, an employee or an authorized representative of the employees must be allowed to accompany the inspector through the plant. Workers should be aware, however, that the Department of Labor has ruled in two cases that companies may refuse to pay employees for time spent in walk-around inspections with federal inspectors. Employee representatives should make it clear to management *before* any inspection takes place that they consider it their right under the act to be paid while accompanying a federal inspector on a walk-around inspection.

These rulings on walk-around pay could especially handicap unorganized workers in securing the protection that was granted them under the Occupational Safety and Health Act. Unorganized labor is further disadvantaged by the fact that nearly all of the act's provisions are aimed at organized labor's participation, although only one-third of those workers covered by the law are unionized. For these reasons, health and safety could become an effective organizing issue at nonunionized plants and thereby increase the pressure on employers to provide a hazard-free workplace for all.

SAMPLE REQUEST FOR INSPECTION: GENERAL DUTY

Date

Regional Administrator
John F. Kennedy Federal Bldg.
Government Center, 17th Floor
Boston, Mass. 02203

Dear Sir:

I would like to request an inspection of my workplace under the "general duty" grounds of the 1970 Occupational

Safety and Health Act. The authorized representative at our plant is Dave Deegan, and his phone number is 234-5678.

The plant is owned by the ABC Company and is located at 1234 James Street, North Battle, Massachusetts 02203. At this plant we make asbestos wallboard. The asbestos particles are in the air in the whole plant. There are 230 workers at this plant and we all have to breathe this asbestos in the air eight hours a day.

The only protection we have against the asbestos fibers, which are known to be deadly, is an exhaust system that is 6 years old. It did not help much when it was new, and has had no maintenance since it was installed. In the last 5 years 10 workers in this plant have died of asbestosis and countless others have some type of lung disorder.

All attempts to get management to install newer, more efficient exhaust systems have gotten no response. There has been no official inspection made here in 9 years and this is the first request that has been made under the new law.

To my knowledge there is no standard at the moment for allowable amounts of asbestos particles in the air, but obviously the employees at this plant are in danger. For this reason my request is based on the grounds of general duty.

I would also like my name left off of any copies that are made of this request, and of any other documents that relate to this request. In the event that no inspection is made in response to this request, I also expect a written letter from you explaining why you denied my request.

Respectfully,

/s/ W. Power
W. Power

SAMPLE REQUEST FOR INSPECTION:
VIOLATION OF A STANDARD

                                           Date

Regional Administrator
506 Second Avenue
1804 Smith Tower Bldg.
Seattle, Washington 98014

Dear Sir:

I would like to request an inspection of my workplace. I believe that there is a violation of a standard set under the 1970 Occupational Safety and Health Act. The authorized representative at our plant is Bob Gardner and his phone number is 234-6698.

The plant is owned by the M. M. Meat Company, and is located at 318 6th Street, Stanton, Oregon 98771. One of the operations carried out in the plant is meat grinding. Usually about 25 people work in the north wing where the grinding machine is located.

Members of our union became aware of the dangers of noise pollution and we bought a noise measuring device. We have found that the noise level in the north wing is 112 decibels when the grinder is operating. The current standard says that a worker can be exposed to 112 decibels for only 24 minutes per day. However, the grinder is on at least 4 hours of each 8 hour shift. Therefore we have many people exposed to much more noise than the law allows.

There are no earplugs or other safety devices provided to protect the workers in the north wing from the noise of the grinder. We have asked the company to lower the noise level in the north wing, but they say that it is technically impossible. The machine has been in use for 6 months, and the last state inspection for noise was made before this machine was put into use.

I am requesting this inspection because of a violation of the noise standard. In the event that there is no inspection in response to this request, I expect a written letter from you explaining why you denied my request.

Respectfully,

/s/ A. Louden
A. Louden

SAMPLE REQUEST FOR INSPECTION:
IMMINENT DANGER

Date

Regional Administrator
Penn Square Bldg., Room 410
Juniper & Filbert Streets
Philadelphia, Pa. 19107

Dear Sir:

I would like to request an immediate inspection of my workplace under the 1970 Occupational Safety and Health Act. I believe that workers are in imminent danger of serious physical harm and death. The authorized representative is Norman Gurwitz, and his phone number is 293-8613.

The plant is owned by the Battery Chemical Company, and is located at 4420 Smithville Road, Cottingham, Virginia 20650. One of the chemical operations at the plant requires the use of mercury. It has been known that mercury is dangerous, and for this reason the company has transferred men out of the "mercury cell" whenever they show signs of mercury poisoning. Normally 40 workers are assigned to the "cell" at a time, but there are over 250 men who have worked there at one time or another.

Last week 2 men were hospitalized with symptoms of mercury poisoning and one of them has since died. It is for this reason that I feel that all the workers who have been in the "mercury cell" may be in imminent danger. If so then this part of the plant should be closed down until proper protection can be provided.

The "mercury cell" has been operating for 7 years and there have been 5 state inspections during this period. Whenever an inspector arrived it always seemed to be the day that the "cell" was operating at 10% capacity. No violation has ever been found.

The only monitoring that is done of mercury levels is done by the company. They test mercury levels in employees' urine. This information has never been given to the employees.

I would like my name left off of any copies that are made of this request, and of any other documents that relate to this request. In the event that there is not an immediate inspection made in response to this request, I also expect an immediate written letter from you explaining why you denied my request.

Respectfully,

/s/ Richard Schultz
Richard Schultz

Fighting Noise: An Occupational Health Case Study*

Anyone who works in a place that is usually noisy or where there are occasional but very loud noises risks loss of hearing. That is bad enough by itself, but he may also risk increased tension, headaches, circulatory, cardiovascular, or neurological irregularities. Although noise has been the subject of increasing concern by environmentalists and by physicians, little has been done to reduce dangerous noise levels in factories and plants. Management ordinarily is not particularly concerned about noise in the workplace, and considers it a necessary and inevitable part of the job. Unlike accidents, in which immediate injury occurs, noise inflicts its damages gradually. Employers rarely have to pay for hearing loss suffered by workers, and it may be difficult to prove that noise at work was the cause of an employee's deafness. Workers themselves are not often concerned about noise: they may not know about its dangers, they may have become so used to high noise levels that they do not really notice them, or they, too, may think that noise is part of the job.

Only aware, concerned workers, acting alone or supported by their unions, can begin to quiet the noisy work environment. There are several steps one can take.

First, an informal survey of the workplace will reveal

* This project is based on material in *Noise and Your Job*, and is used here with thanks to Urban Planning Aid, Inc.

the areas where noise is loudest. Workers in those areas should be asked if they experience any of the following problems:

1. Workers have trouble talking to each other or have to shout to be heard,

2. Ears ring after being in a work area,

3. A temporary loss of hearing occurs after exposure to noise.

If any of these is true of your workplace, there is probably too much noise; the next step is to get your union to measure the amount of noise with a sound meter. Noise is measured in decibels (dB). The decibel scale is arranged so that each increase of 10 units means 10 times as much noise, that is 80 dB is *10 times* more noise than 70 dB and 90 dB is *100 times* more sound pressure than 70 dB. Here are some examples of the decibel ratings of different sounds:

Ordinary conversation	60	dB
Busy street traffic	75	dB
Office tabulating machines	80	dB
Linotype machines	88–91	dB
Subway train, twenty feet away	90	dB
Can manufacturing plant	100	dB
Newspaper printing press	102–108	dB
Caterpillar tractor, idling	104	dB
Circular saw	105–116	dB
Drills, shovels and trucks in operation	108	dB
Woodworking shop	110	dB
Sandblasting	112	dB
Riveting steel tank	130	dB
Jet with afterburner on, fifty feet away	140	dB

A federal inspector can be called in from the Occupational Safety and Health Administration to check to see if there is a violation of federal noise standards. On October 18, 1972, OSHA issued the following standards, which are now in effect:

Duration of Exposure Per Day, in Hours	Maximum Permissible Sound Level in Decibels
8	90
6	92
4	95
3	97
2	100
1½	102
1	105
½	110
¼ or less	115

Unfortunately, federal enforcement in this area has been slow, and if a violation is found, the company can appeal before correcting the trouble.

This is a long process, so workers must be prepared to take action on their own. There is much that can be done. Contact a medical, legal, or public interest group to get advice on noise problems and what can be done about them. If you do not know of a local organization, write Industrial Health and Safety Project, Urban Planning Aid, 639 Massachusetts Avenue, Cambridge, Massachusetts 02139, or the Health Research Group, 2000 P Street, N.W., Suite 708, Washington, D.C. 20036. If these groups cannot help, they know others who will.

Try to arrange for noncompany health specialists to tour the workplace. After the tour the health specialist should be invited to speak at a union meeting to explain the medical consequences of too high noise levels. Many people never realize how injurious noise is.

Get trained audiologists (hearing experts) to test workers to determine whether hearing loss has occurred. The Health Research Group runs a clearinghouse for volunteer audiologists from around the country who are willing to advise workers on hearing problems; many universities also have speech-hearing departments with students who might volunteer to do testing. The results of the tests should be tabulated and presented to management.

During collective bargaining negotiations, specific requests for improved conditions can be made to management. Workers should demand that the company provide yearly hearing tests for workers in noisy areas to ensure that they are protected before suffering significant damage. Workers should dismiss arguments that if they cannot stand the working conditions they should go elsewhere. Many machines now are engineered to meet federal noise levels. Also it is possible to lower noise levels by running machines at lower speeds, using plastic gears, erecting baffles to deflect and absorb noise or by installing sound absorbing insulation or a muffler. Workers can be rotated so they spend less time in noisy areas.

The same tactics used to combat noise can work against other hazards of the work environment, such as dust, chemicals, and other harmful substances. It is up to workers to take the lead to protect their own safety and health. A fat pay check and good fringe benefits are worth fighting for, but it's also nice to live to enjoy them. Along with other contract clauses, unions should bargain for specific safeguards for health and safety. Some important areas in which to promulgate written guarantees are the following:

—Safety Committee composed of equal numbers of union and management and a chairman chosen by the union in alternating months;

—Specific arbitration clause for health and safety grievances;

—Mandatory pay for union members who represent labor during inspections ("walk-around pay");

—Specific clauses governing work conditions, for example, noise, ventilation, dust, etc.;

—Surveillance and monitoring of employee exposure to occupational hazards and notifying employees of results;

—Labeling of the contents of all substances used according to chemical name;

—Posting of occupational hazard notices in the workplace.

A manual detailing a plan for local worker action on noise problems, based on the actual experience of a newspaper pressman's union fighting noise in their pressroom, can be obtained for twenty-five cents (for mailing costs) from the Health Research Group (address above).

Hospital Projects

Hospitals are big business. They collected approximately $30 billion in fees during 1971, most of it paid to private, nonprofit hospitals governed by boards of trustees largely closed off from public participation or scrutiny. In addition, there are public hospitals whose trustees are accountable to public officials, and a growing number of hospitals run for profit. In these, compassion takes a second place to the earnings ratio.

Many critics of health services claim that hospitals are run as private fiefdoms for the benefit of doctors, administrators, and trustees, while ignoring patients' needs. Herbert S. Denenberg, the insurance commissioner of Pennsylvania, supports this contention. "If the public knew what was going on in hospitals and how much they are gouging, they'd be outraged."

The projects contained in this section touch on a variety of aspects of hospital care, from cost and management to the adequacy of facilities and services. Their common link is that they all attempt to engender greater citizen participation in hospital affairs. But they are only a start. Continuous monitoring of hospital affairs by consumer groups, health organizations, and reformist medical associations is necessary, if the patient's welfare is to become paramount. A more extensive manual for citizens interested in improving hospitals is available from the Health Research Group, 2000 P St., N.W., Washington, D.C. 20036.

PREPARATION OF A SHOPPER'S GUIDE TO HOSPITALS

> Shopping for a hospital may not be in vogue, but greater dissemination of information and wide public awareness might contribute to more hospital economy.
>
> —Herbert S. Denenberg,
> Insurance Commissioner of the
> Commonwealth of Pennsylvania

Most people are not in a position to choose the hospital they depend upon for health care. For the medically indigent, there is only the municipal or county hospital. Those who have private medical insurance or can afford to pay for private hospital care seldom have greater choices, mainly because their doctor has privileges only at one hospital. Nevertheless, even though few may "shop" for hospitals, the information contained in a shopper's guide is helpful to consumers in several important ways. First, it serves to educate the public about the actual costs involved in medical care. Second, by making this information public, the guide may put pressure on hospital administrators and Blue Cross officials to hold down hospital costs. Third, if citizens begin to see themselves as "consumers" as well as "patients" they may begin to demand higher quality service and greater responsiveness from hospital administrators.

A Shopper's Guide to Hospitals is simply a descriptive breakdown of facilities, services, and costs at local hospitals. The preparation of a Shopper's Guide is a good initial project to pave the way for more consumer participation in the health care system. The first guide of this kind was published in Pennsylvania and a free copy is available from

Herbert S. Denenberg, Insurance Commissioner, Harrisburg, Pennsylvania.* Commissioner Denenberg's Guide can serve as a model, but additional information should be included to suit local conditions. The following are the first two listings in his Guide. The remaining listings follow the same pattern.

Citizens can find information concerning hospital costs in the American Hospital Association's annual booklet entitled *Hospital Statistics*. It is available from the AHA (840 North Lake Shore Drive, Chicago, Illinois 60611). Additional information concerning health care costs may be obtained from the state office of Blue Cross, from the state Department of Health, from the U.S. Department of Health, Education, and Welfare, from hospital information offices, or from reports by investigative journalists. For example, the April 22, 1972, issue of the *National Journal* reported that in the five-year period ending June, 1971, hospital daily service charges increased 96 percent, operating room charges 77 percent, and X-ray services 35 percent. One of the best investigative reports on hospitals, *The Hospital Business*, appeared in a six-part series by Ron Kessler of *The Washington Post*, October 29 through November 3, 1972. Reprints are available free from the *Post*'s Public

* Commissioner Denenberg has also published comparable guides to health insurance and unnecessary surgery.

Name and Address of Hospital	Per Diem Charge	Per Diem Cost Nonmaternity
*Abington Memorial Hospital Abington, Pa.	$ 86.83	$84.00
*Albert Einstein Medical Center Northern Division York & Tabor Rds. Philadelphia, Pa.	125.89	84.00

Relations Office (1150 Fifteenth Street, N.W., Washington, D.C. 20005).

Once the local data is compiled into a guide, it should be released to the news media at a special press conference. To heighten the impact, background information should be gathered to illustrate the dramatic rise in hospital costs and the consequent increase in the cost of medical insurance over the past ten or twenty years. Relevant comments by specialists on hospital costs will further add to the news value and authority of the report. Finally, the report should be mimeographed and made available to the public free or for a nominal cost to cover printing and postage.

INVESTIGATION OF A HOSPITAL BOARD OF TRUSTEES

Theoretically, a hospital board of trustees is the group most capable of changing hospital policies to make them more responsive to consumers. The board, as the governing body of the hospital corporation, makes basic policy decisions, such as what kinds of health programs the hospital should have and what equipment it must buy. It not only

Per Diem Cost Maternity	Occupancy	Average Length of Stay	Total Bed Capacity
$110.00	91.4	7.5 days	471
115.00	91.4	10.1 days	737

controls the budget, but appoints hospital administrators and members of the medical staff. It also reviews for final approval the recommendations of the medical staff for physician appointments and privileges at the hospital. These are critical powers. For example, a decision to buy an expensive new piece of equipment for the operating room rather than to outfit a community clinic may decisively affect health care in the community. Should fees be increased? Should special emphasis be placed on hiring minorities and women? Should health programs be instituted for low-income consumers? Decisions such as these determine who the hospital will serve.

Unfortunately, many hospital boards are out of touch with consumer needs. They are more interested in representing their own private interests or those of local politicians, businessmen, or the medical profession than those of the patients. Most boards do not have any representatives of patients, workers or hospital staff members. A recent investigation of Herrick Hospital in Berkeley, California, for example, showed that Herrick's thirteen-member board consisted of five doctors, two hospital administrators, a banker, a lawyer, a lawyer's wife, an insurance executive, a businessman, and a single community leader. The nonvoting advisory board set up to represent the community was not much better. Its membership included a drug and hospital supply company executive, the manager of a chemical company, a department store executive, an architect, a former hospital administrator, three elected officials, and three civic leaders. By background and training, these people were ill-equipped to represent the needs and interests of the substantial student, black, and working class communities in Berkeley.

Many hospital boards have members with open conflicts of interest.* Ron Kessler's investigation of Washington

---

* The *Hospital Law Manual*, a standard reference work for hospital attorneys, states that a conflict of interest occurs when a hospital trustee does business with the hospital, automatically giving him conflicting interests on both sides of the transaction.

Hospital Center revealed numerous clear-cut cases of conflicts of interest. For years the hospital maintained large deposits (as high as $1.8 million) in a checking account at the American Security and Trust Company. Kessler conservatively estimated that the hospital forfeited at least $50,000 a year in lost interest payments because of this arrangement. Not coincidentally, the hospital's financial affairs were managed by a vice-president of American Security.

Kessler turned up many more abuses. At various times ten of the thirty-eight trustees were found to have conflicts of interest. These ranged from funneling the hospital's stock transactions through a stockbroker who was the son-in-law of a trustee to acceptance of free care by trustees. In each case, trustees, their businesses, or relatives benefited at the expense of the hospital and ultimately at the expense of the consumer forced to bear the higher costs.

To discover conflicts of interest as extensive as those uncovered in Washington requires months of painstaking sifting of records, interviews, and analysis; Ron Kessler is an experienced investigative reporter. But a citizens group interested in hospital management can perform a valuable service merely by analyzing the make-up of the board of trustees of local hospitals. More than likely this analysis will reveal the same pattern as the board of Herrick. The initial question, therefore, is to determine what interests board members actually represent. One obvious solution is to secure more balanced representation. This is more easily prescribed than accomplished.

Public hospitals are usually run by government agencies. Pressure generated through elected officials or an attempt to turn the quality of hospital care into a campaign issue

---

People who work for or own substantial stock in health insurance companies or surgical or medical supply firms that do business with the hospital; bankers in whose banks hospital funds are deposited; lawyers who are also retained as hospital counsel are people who have actual or potential conflicts of interest.

can sometimes change the make-up and policies of a public hospital. If the hospital is private, the board is probably self-perpetuating and is not nearly so susceptible to public pressure. In either case, however, citizen activists can take several steps to make hospital boards more representative and thus, one hopes, more responsive to community needs.

First, a citizens group should request greater representation of consumer interests on hospital boards. Second, they should build an alliance with other community groups, members of the hospital staff, hospital employees unions, and concerned professionals working in the hospital. Third, they should present their suggested reforms to the present board to give it the opportunity to make the desired changes on its own. For example, if the Herrick Board expanded from thirteen to twenty-five members by adding twelve community actively participating representatives, the demand for more community input might have been satisfied. If the board remains unresponsive, or dismisses the request outright, citizen pressure must be brought to bear on it. Pressure can be exerted by enlisting the aid of the local press and religious and political leaders, calling in responsible government agencies, holding citizen hearings, or conducting consumer picketing. At Herrick, a table was set up outside the hospital to collect complaints from patients and to dispense information to the community. Although the citizen activists at Herrick did not succeed completely in restructuring the hospital board and reforming procedures, they did win several important concessions.

If conflicts of interests are discovered, they should be exposed and the resignations of offending board members should be demanded. The mere threat of exposure may persuade those with genuine conflicts to resign rather than face hostile publicity; otherwise legal action may be necessary.

Unions, staff, or professionals within the hospital can apply pressure of their own. For example, expansion of clinical services to the working class might be part of a union's contract negotiations. A petition signed by hospital doctors opposed to the board's policies is bound to have an effect on board decisions, especially if the press is informed of the doctor's actions.

Board representation, while important because of its control over a hospital's policies, is not the only avenue for action open to a citizens group intent on reform. Even if a campaign for broader representation is thwarted, a citizens group may be able to force specific changes using other points of leverage. Some ways to do this are outlined in the following projects.

EVALUATION OF EMERGENCY SERVICES

> In 1965, 52 million accidental injuries killed 107,000, temporarily disabled over 10 million, and permanently impaired 400,000 American citizens at a cost of $18 billion. This neglected epidemic of a modern society is the nation's most important environmental health problem. It is the leading cause of death in the first half of life's span.
>
> —National Academy of Sciences

The statistics on deaths, injuries, and disabilities reveal only part of the story. Accident patients are also a serious drain on hospital resources. According to HEW, they take up four times more space than cancer patients do.

A hospital study cannot reduce the number of accidental injuries but it can seek ways to upgrade the facilities for treatment of them. Presumably, if better care is offered to accident victims, the number of fatalities and permanent disabilities can be reduced, even if the number of injuries remains constant. Better emergency care is also likely to reduce the time spent in the hospital.

Ambulance Service

Ambulance service is not usually provided by hospitals, but by fire departments, volunteer services, undertakers, or profit-making companies. Although technically beyond the bounds of a hospital study, ambulance service is a key link in the chain of emergency services, with significant indirect effects on hospitals. For example, an improvement in the ability of ambulance technicians to handle cardiac arrests may well increase the life expectancy of heart-attack victims more significantly than a comparable improvement in hospital cardiac facilities. Other accidents and diseases follow a similar pattern. The sooner a victim's condition can be stabilized, the better the chance of survival and the less likely the chance of permanent disability.

After years of neglect, the federal government in the mid-sixties finally began a serious effort to improve ambulance services. One major impetus to federal involvement was the carnage on the nation's highways which by 1965 accounted for 50,000 deaths—half of all accidental deaths—and the hospitalization of over a million and a half citizens. Under a Department of Transportation program, the federal government will pay 50 percent of the cost of an ambulance up to $6,750, and 50 percent of all approved equipment for the vehicle. The details of this program are explained in the Highway Safety Program manual, *Emergency Medical Services*, Vol. II. It can be ordered from the National Highway Traffic Safety Administration, General Services Division, Washington, D.C. 20590.

States and local communities have been slow to respond to the federal initiative; citizen activists are needed to exert constructive pressure to better ambulance services. To evaluate ambulance service in your community, you should use the *Guide for Conducting State and Community Surveys of Ambulance Services and Hospital Emergency Departments,* available from the Health Services and Mental Health Administration, Division of Emergency Health Services, 5600 Fishers Lane, Rockville, Maryland 20852.

While this pamphlet provides no measurement scale with which to judge the level of compliance with the suggested standards, it does provide survey forms and questionnaires. Evaluative standards can be found in an article entitled "Essential Equipment for Ambulances" in the May, 1970, issue of the *Bulletin of the American College of Surgeons,* or in *Medical Requirements for Ambulance Design and Equipment* (available from the Division of Medical Sciences, National Academy of Sciences, 2101 Constitution Avenue, N.W., Washington, D.C. 20418) or *Emergency Medical Services, Recommendations for an Approach,* pages 51–57 (available from the American College of Surgeons, 55 East Erie Street, Chicago, Illinois 60611).

Using the survey and all or some of the materials containing suggested standards, citizen activists can evaluate a community ambulance service with respect to ambulance design, equipment, and competence of ambulance technicians. A separate study is required to evaluate speed of service.

Emergency Rooms

Ambulance services are the first link in the chain of emergency medical care. Emergency rooms are obviously the second. The study of Herrick Hospital in Berkeley, referred to above, centered on Herrick's emergency room. Citizen activists in Berkeley, led by the Medical Committee for Human Rights, found that Herrick's emergency room discriminated against the poor and subjected many patients to intolerably long delays before receiving care. Consumer groups in other cities have complained that emergency room personnel discriminate on the basis of color, language ability, and dress. There are numerous other problems associated with emergency rooms, some of which are described in *The Emergency Room,* a pamphlet available from the

Health Law Project, University of Pennsylvania School of Law, 133 South 36th Street, Philadelphia, Pennsylvania 19104.

An investigation of a hospital emergency room can look into two distinct problems: the adequacy of the facilities and the quality of the treatment. The first investigation can be conducted in the same way as the ambulance evaluation. The Health Services and Mental Health Administration booklet, useful for investigating ambulance services (see p. 106), contains a survey of emergency room facilities. The results of the survey can be measured against standards for emergency rooms outlined in the following pamphlets: *Categorization of Hospital Emergency Capabilities*, American Medical Association, 535 North Dearborn Street, Chicago, Illinois 60610, $0.45; *Emergency Medical Services, Recommendations for an Approach* (pp. 67–71), American College of Surgeons, 55 East Erie Street, Chicago, Illinois 60611.

Once the condition of emergency room facilities is determined, the more difficult question of the quality of care can be taken up. Even though a citizens group may have difficulty judging strictly medical questions, such as how a fracture was set or whether one surgical technique or another should have been employed, there are ways laymen can play a role in judging the quality of health care. Laymen are perfectly capable of judging whether waiting periods are unreasonable, whether the emergency room is clean, and whether patients themselves feel satisfied. There are computer analyses on the cost of various kinds of surgery and evaluations of various medical practices which the laymen can understand. They are distributed by the Commission on Professional and Hospital Activities, 168 Green Road, Ann Arbor, Michigan 48104. Each treatment can be measured against these standards of care.

An investigation of the quality of care, requires more skill and takes more time than a simple facility survey. The first step is to devise a methodology for the investigation. Questionnaires can be distributed to staff and professionals within the emergency room. Every effort must be taken to avoid alienating the staff by involving activist staff members from the start in planning the project. At Herrick Hospital, where this was not done, the staff felt so threatened by the citizens' activity that initially they refused all cooperation. A survey table can also be set up near the emergency room with questionnaires to determine patients' reaction to the quality of care.

Step two is to compare the emergency room of the hospital being studied with emergency rooms of other hospitals. Although this comparison may prove nothing, if all of the rooms are on the same level, the comparison is more likely to reveal differences that will point the way to areas needing closer study.

Step three, if the services are found deficient, is to meet with the hospital administrator, the board of trustees, or the advisory board of the hospital to make suggestions for improvement. If these are accepted, the investigation has accomplished its purpose. If they are dismissed or rejected, however, stronger action must be taken. A determined group of citizens should be able to induce a local government agency or a legislative committee to convene hearings on the quality of emergency care. If the government won't hold hearings, activists can schedule their own citizen hearings (see page 179). Public opinion can have a significant impact on hospitals.

If public pressure fails to change hospital policies, stronger measures are needed. Inadequate equipment may violate regulations of the state Department of Health. Certainly, if the services offered are below acceptable standards, patients may have grounds to sue the hospital for negligence. Citizen groups can also apply pressure through participation in accreditation proceedings.

HOW TO PARTICIPATE IN HOSPITAL ACCREDITATION

After investigating costs, employment practices, facilities, or delivery of service in a hospital, several avenues for action are open to the citizen activist seeking improved health care. Between 1946 and 1948 almost every state passed laws to license hospitals. This flurry of legislative activity was occasioned by passage of the Hill-Burton Act which required all states wishing federal funds for hospital construction to pass legislation "providing compliance with minimum standards of maintenance and operation." Most states established minimum standards that dealt mainly with facilities, not quality of care, and provided almost no enforcement powers; nevertheless, their existence offers citizens a potential action tool. Appointment of a reformer to head the state Department of Health might, for example, mean stronger enforcement; if citizen pressure for better health care continues to build, the demand for reform may be too great to resist. Michigan and New York recently passed tougher provisions dealing with both facilities and quality of care. Both states have established inspection teams to enforce their standards. Similar laws should be promoted in other states.

There is still another action tool which is more accessible to citizen activists than state licensing laws. Every two years many hospitals are visited by the Joint Commission on Accreditation of Hospitals (JCAH), composed of representatives from the American Medical Association, the American Hospital Association, the American College of Surgeons, and the American College of Physicians. The commission is a private body set up to inspect hospitals on a voluntary basis. At one time JCAH accreditation was solely a matter of prestige within the medical fraternity. Now it is more important because accreditation by JCAH is a prerequisite factor in qualifying the hospital for certification under Medicare. Loss of accreditation is a clear signal to health officials and the general public that the hospital is in trouble and that upgrading is needed.

Unfortunately, JCAH accreditation inspections are as weak or weaker than state enforcement of licensing standards. The director of JCAH, Dr. John D. Porterfield, revealed the organization's bias when he was asked why JCAH did not make surprise inspections of hospitals. He replied, "While the possibility of a surprise visit might keep hospitals more constantly on the *qui vive*, the practice has never been followed by the Joint Commission primarily because the JCAH considers the visit by its survey personnel more of a *consultation than an evaluation*." [Emphasis added.] Given this attitude and the fact that nineteen out of the twenty members of the JCAH executive board are doctors, it is no wonder that the inspection for accreditation has more often than not been a rubber-stamp procedure.

Recently, however, consumer pressure and demands by concerned hospital personnel have forced JCAH into a more active posture. In a demonstration of toughness, JCAH revoked the accreditation of both St. Louis City Hospital and Boston City Hospital and granted one-year provisional accreditations to Cook County General, Detroit General, and D.C. General hospitals. Later the revocations were reduced to provisional accreditations, but even this retreat cannot obscure the fact that at last JCAH had taken action.

Citizen activists should take advantage of JCAH's new posture to press their demands for better health care. Community groups have a right to meet with the JCAH accrediting representative to press their case in person. Written reports from citizens become part of the inspection records. The consumer cause will be furthered if medical personnel within the hospital join in presenting evidence of poor facilities or inadequate care. In preparation for the JCAH visit in 1970, the resident doctors of D.C. General issued a statement detailing a variety of hospital problems. In an accompanying press release, the residents complained,

"The medical wards constantly run 75 to 100 beds over capacity. We are turning sick people out in the streets to make room for people who are even more ill." The resident's action created a climate for reform which JCAH could not ignore.

Citizens interested in upgrading hospital standards would do well to read "Regulation of Quality of Care in Hospitals: The Need for Change" by William Worthington and Laurens Silver, in *Law and Contemporary Problems*, vol. 35 (1970). This publication should be available at all law libraries and most major public libraries.

For more information on hospital accreditation, an excellent paper has been prepared by the Health Law Project at the University of Pennsylvania School of Law (133 South 36th Street, Philadelphia, Pennsylvania 19104) entitled *The Accreditation of Hospitals: A Guide for Health Consumers and Workers*. It describes in detail how to participate in the accreditation process. Additional information can be obtained by writing to the Joint Commission on Accreditation of Hospitals, 645 North Michigan Avenue, Chicago, Illinois 60611.

Another source of valuable information about medical facilities has recently become available to the public. A 1972 amendment to the Medicare section of the Social Security Act (42 U.S.C.A. 1395) provides that surveys conducted by HEW of hospitals, laboratories, clinics, extended care facilities, and other institutions to determine Medicare-Medicaid compliance be made available to the public at the district office of the Social Security Administration within ninety days of the completion of the survey. This enables citizens to obtain detailed government reports which they can use directly or as evidence to substantiate their own information when they testify before or submit a report to JCAH.

How to Turn Blue Cross and Blue Shield into Consumer Advocates

Richard F. Upton is an attorney in Concord, New Hampshire. One of his clients is Blue Cross. Mr. Upton, according to Mavis Doyle of the Vermont Press Bureau, recently received a fee "for representing Blue Cross in its efforts to get a rate increase from the general public." Wearing a different hat, Mr. Upton serves as a representative of the general public on the Blue Cross Board. Theoretically, the public interest is to *reduce* Blue Cross rates, yet Mr. Upton was advocating an *increase*. When asked about this conflict of interest, Mr. Upton replied, "I figure I am speaking for the public interest when I am speaking for the company."

The investigation that turned up Mr. Upton's curious dual allegiance was conducted by the Vermont Public Interest Research Group (VPIRG). At the conclusion of their study, VPIRG charged that Blue Cross–Blue Shield was managed by boards of directors riddled with conflicts of interest. Many directors were found to have substantial economic interests that were benefited rather than harmed by rising medical costs. VPIRG recommended that the insurance commissioners of New Hampshire and Vermont take steps to ensure that consumer interest be adequately represented. Responding in part to consumer pressure, the Insurance Commissioners of Vermont and New Hampshire in February, 1973, refused to approve a rate increase for Blue Cross–Blue Shield. Referring to board members' conflicts of interest, Commissioner John Durkin of New Hampshire denounced the "sweetheart" relationship between the board and the companies.

In Pennsylvania, Insurance Commissioner Denenberg has taken the lead in trying to make Blue Cross–Blue Shield responsive to consumer interests. His recommendations are not limited to curtailing rising health care costs. Because Blue Cross–Blue Shield represent millions of people and because they contract only with certain hospitals, they have enormous power and influence over the provision of health care. They could, for example, save consumers millions of dollars annually by requiring all contracting hospitals to use generic drugs rather than brand names whenever possible. (See Prescription Drug Project, page 70.) Commissioner Denenberg has drawn up a list of thirty-three suggested contract provisions that can be included in every Blue Cross contract. They are reprinted below as a guide to citizen activists. Using these materials, citizen groups can begin to question hospital administrators to discover whether their hospitals have adopted the same or similar provisions. The insurance commissioner of the state can be urged by citizen groups to refuse requests for Blue Cross rate increases unless hospitals agree to follow these money-saving suggestions.

1. *Duplicative and Underutilized Facilities and Services.*
   It is generally agreed that there are many duplicative and underutilized hospital facilities and services. Perhaps the classic example is open-heart surgery and certain types of hospital services, such as the pediatric and maternity division.
   Some agency might be selected to determine which duplicative and underutilized facilities and services should be phased out and which new ones should be authorized for the future.
   The Blue Cross–hospital contract negotiations should consider new approaches to the elimination of unnecessary and duplicative services.
2. *Elimination of Unsafe and Otherwise Substandard Beds.*
   Blue Cross subscribers should not be called on to pay for the use of unsafe and unsuitable hospital beds.

Blue Cross and the hospitals should consider not reimbursing for such beds and closing them down altogether. Certainly, in areas where there are excessive beds, there is no reason for not closing down beds and hospitals which are unsafe or otherwise unsuitable.

Some hospitals can be closed altogether. Other hospitals can close some units, and perhaps still maintain adequate beds by use of preadmission testing, the seven-day work week, and similar measures.

3. *Financing of Residents and Interns.*

The costs of residents and interns, as part of hospitals' reimbursable costs, have been rapidly escalating, and is a substantial cost factor. In medical school hospitals, this cost may run as high as ten dollars per day per patient and the end is not in sight.

One possibility is the transfer of this cost to the physicians themselves. Other possibilities should be explored. For example, some maximum limit for the costs of residents and interns might be established.

4. *Limitation on the Number of Employees.*

Many hospitals have increased their employee force, sometimes without any apparent increase in patient care. There is now no effective limitation on unnecessary personnel increases.

The contract should consider provisions to control increases in personnel and perhaps even rollbacks on present personnel. An agency might be selected to authorize any additional employees, including salaried physicians.

5. *Depreciation.*

Reimbursing for depreciation, as a hospital cost, has been a hotly debated question for some time. Some believe depreciation as a cost should be sharply limited or eliminated altogether. The cost implications of depreciations are substantial. The depreciation expenses at some hospitals may run ten dollars per day or more, and the aggregate bill for depreciation is sharply rising.

It is clearly time to reconsider this issue carefully.

6. *Prospective Rating.*

There are inherent weaknesses in reimbursing on the basis of open-ended costs.

Consideration should be given to some form of prospective rating so a hospital's expenditures for a given period can be fixed in advance.

Consideration might also be given to determining a specified aggregate annual amount of money payable by all Blue Cross subscribers, which would then be appropriately distributed to all participating facilities for all services to be rendered.

7. *Budgetary Review.*

Each hospital should operate on a budget, and these budgets should be submitted to Blue Cross in advance for prior review.

Hospitals, whose costs are out of line when compared to similar institutions, could then be so advised and appropriate corrective measures taken.

Consideration should be given to all methods of advance budgetary review and authorization.

8. *Adoption of Cost-Saving Devices*

Hospitals have not taken advantage of proven cost-saving devices, such as preadmission testing and graded care.

The contract should require such economies rather than merely offer incentives for their implementation. Consideration should be given to all such economies that can be built into the contract.

9. *Ancillary Services Provided by Physicians.*

The compensation arrangement for the services of ancillary specialists—anesthesiologists, pathologists, and radiologists—often produce fantastic incomes. The Board of Trustees of some hospitals may not even be aware of the income produced by some of these percentage arrangements.

Consideration should be given to a contractual arrangement requiring disclosure of the actual levels of compensation produced by these arrangements. Boards of Trustees might consider setting a maximum dollar amount on any compensation arrangement. Another possibility is to place all hospital-based physicians on fixed dollar salaries.

10. *Denial of Reimbursement for Costs of Some Organizations.*

Hospitals are reimbursed for their dues paid to such organizations as the Delaware Valley Hospital Council and the Hospital Association of Pennsylvania.

Consideration should be given to denial of reimbursement when dues are paid to more than one organization that may render the same services.

11. *Consumer Control of Hospitals.*

Our health delivery system is desperately in need of more consumer input. This is true of Blue Cross as well as the hospitals.

Consideration should be given to an appropriate contractual arrangement to assure adequate consumer representation on hospital boards.

12. *The Hospital: Country Club or Open Institution?*

Every step should be taken to subject the health delivery system to the influences of competition.

One important step in this direction would be authorization of physicians to practice in any hospital rather than imposing country-club limitations on what physicians can practice in what hospital.

Consideration should be given to creating an open-door policy for all physicians at all hospitals.

13. *Generic Drugs.*

It has been estimated that drug bills might be cut as much as 60 to 95 percent by the use of generic rather than brand name drugs.

One possibility is to have all Blue Cross hospitals follow the procedures already used in several major medical institutions. There the doctor prescribes the drug under the brand name he knows, on a prescription blank that carries a printed legend over the space for the doctor's signature that says the pharmacist may substitute a less expensive brand where available and identical chemically.

14. *Reimbursement for General Management Surveys.*

Blue Cross contracts may now provide for reimbursement for projects for design and implementation of more effective systems and procedures for furnishing quality patient care.

Such provisions should be broadened to include general management surveys and to otherwise obtain consultation on the basic issues of hospital management.

15. *Incentives for Cost-Savings Programs.*

Various incentives are included in Blue Cross contracts for certain cost-savings programs, such as pre-admission testing.

In view of the urgent necessity for economies, consideration should be given to making these cost-savings programs mandatory and doing away with related incentive payments.

16. *Better Accounting for Excluded Research Costs.*

Blue Cross does not directly reimburse for research costs. There is reason to believe, however, that research costs may indirectly be commingled with patient care and thus become reimbursable for Blue Cross. The contract should develop standards to eliminate any reimbursement for research, even if indirect.

17. *Public Disclosure of Information.*

The public is entitled to and interested in full disclosure of financial and operational details relating to hospitals.

The contract should give due consideration to making this information available to the public. For example, the cost per day of a hospital stay, average length of stay, aspects of hospital expenses, and other facts should be disclosed.

18. *Utilization Review.*

There is a great deal of evidence that the utilization

review process is not working effectively and that there is substantial overutilization of hospital facilities.

Consideration should be given to contractual provisions containing new approaches to utilization review. Among suggested variations on the present review process is the inclusion of consumer and financial intermediary representatives on review committees.

19. *Protecting the Patient from Improper Charges.*

The patient is now frequently charged for hospitalization that should never have been ordered in the first place.

In such cases, the hospital should not charge for such services, and arrangements should be made for the physician to pick up the tab in such cases.

Consideration should be given to every possible method of protecting the public from improper charges.

20. *Loss Prevention and Control Programs.*

The casualty insurance industry has developed proven methods for eliminating and minimizing hospital accidents and resulting lawsuits. These lawsuits lead to astronomical costs and insurance premiums, and result in higher Blue Cross premiums.

Consideration should be given to requiring each hospital to implement needed safety measures.

21. *Blue Cross Guarantees of Hospital Bad Debts.*

The Blue Cross contract may now compensate hospitals for bad debts resulting from the inability to collect deductibles, coinsurance exclusions, and similar amounts not paid by the applicable Blue Cross contract.

Consideration should be given to transferring the risk of such bad debts from the Blue Cross Plans to the hospitals.

22. *Effective Date of Contract.*

The economies and efficiencies to be built into the Blue Cross–hospital contract should not be unnecessarily postponed even for a day.

Consideration should be given to as early an effective date as possible.

23. *Participation in Hospital Statistical Agency Activities.*

Hospitals should participate in and use services provided by such organizations as the Professional Activities Studies (PAS) or the Hospitalization Utilization Projects (HUP). These services provide comparative data on utilization. Hospitals should also be required to explain any statistical variations significantly above like hospitals. For example, any higher than average stay in any category of major diagnosis should be explained.

24. *Use of Tests Performed Out of Hospitals.*

Hospitals should agree to accept tests and examinations done outside of hospitals by licensed laboratories. Evidence at the Blue Cross hearings indicated hospitals often needlessly duplicate outside tests and often, without good medical reasons, refuse to accept outside tests. This is so, even when the outside laboratories have quality control equal or better than the hospital's own laboratories. In one case, a doctor on the staff of the hospital indicated he could not even use his own outside tests in his own hospital.

25. *More Uniform Accounting.*

Hospitals should be required to move toward more uniform accounting to make the gathering, exchange and analysis of data easier for Blue Cross and others.

26. *Greater Use of Systems Departments.*

Should every hospital have a systems department to carry out departmental efficiency studies, with annual reports to Blue Cross? As one fiscal intermediary commented: "A systems department (even if only one talented man and a part-time clerk) can usually justify its existence and cost through review of needs and the establishment of goals and responsibilities, and selecting areas for quick investigation and quick pay-off in improvement of efficiency and cash savings."

27. *Strong Budget Committees with Outside Representation.*

Should every hospital have a budget committee, with

outside representatives as well as trustee representatives, and specified composition?

28. *Use of Prudent Buying Practices.*

Special provisions should assure that hospitals are not purchasing merchandise at vastly inflated prices. Evidence at the Blue Cross hearings indicated hospitals may buy such items as scissors, tape measures, and furniture through hospital supply companies at many times the cost of identical equipment through conventional channels. For example, one witness at our hearing indicated "hospital" tape measures might sell for $2.50 and "hospital" scissors for $7.50, but identical products could be bought elsewhere for $0.25 and $2.49 respectively.

29. *Use of Departmental Accounting.*

Under Medicare, either the combination or departmental method of accounting may be used. The combination method of accounting results in overcharging Blue Cross subscribers by many millions of dollars. The departmental method presents a much more accurate accounting method and therefore should be used.

30. *Full Recognition of the Impact of the Wage-Cost Freeze.*

The consumer is entitled to any savings from the wage-price freeze, and any resulting savings should be built into the Blue Cross–hospital contract.

31. *Greater Consumer and Public Information and Participation in Hospital Board Meetings.*

Hospital Board meetings should be announced in advance and should be open to the public.

32. *Blue Cross Should Be More Selective in Deciding What Hospitals to Contract with.*

If a hospital is substandard and does not deliver good-quality medical care, it should not have the benefit of a Blue Cross contract. Blue Cross should establish standards for hospitals and keep raising them from time to time. Eventually, Blue Cross should have contracts only with hospitals which meet all reasonable standards.

33. *Blue Cross Should Have the Right to Put Consultants into Any Hospital.*

It is clear that hospitals often cover up inefficiencies and are afraid to let expert consultants come in to study them. We think that hospitals should open their doors to consultants as long as any extra costs of such consultants are paid by Blue Cross. Moreover, when the need is indicated, the hospital should have to bring in consultants at its own expense.

III

TOWARD EQUAL OPPORTUNITY FOR ALL

The struggle for equality has taken many forms in recent years. Court action broke down the barriers to school integration during the 1950s. When court action alone proved too slow, sit-ins, boycotts, and freedom rides were used to overturn discriminatory practices. Again the courts responded and during the early sixties, desegregation of most public accommodations was accomplished using a combination of these tactics. In 1964 Congress passed a sweeping civil rights law which effectively eliminated the most visible forms of race discrimination in the United States. Unfortunately, the resistance to *real* equality of access and opportunity has been tenacious. While segregated public schools, motels, and eating places no longer flourish, openly protected by state law, they still exist in fact. Moreover, when the Whites Only signs were removed and people began to examine the less obvious, more subtle forms of discrimination, it quickly became apparent that race discrimination cuts across class lines and geographic boundaries. It is a national problem affecting all levels of society.

During the last two decades the attention has focused on obtaining rights for black people. Even though much still remains to be done, the effort has spurred other groups to seek to guarantee their own rights. The projects in this section concentrate on the largest of these efforts, the women's rights movement. This emphasis does not indicate lack of concern for the plight of blacks or other minorities. In fact, since most laws outlaw discrimination on grounds of "race, sex, creed, or national origin," a change of one word, "sex," to "race," or "women" to "black," "chicano" or "Indian" can make many of these same projects suitable for attacking race discrimination.

Of course women are not the only ones affected by sex discrimination. Men, too, have stereotyped roles, are forced to bear heavier economic burdens, and are denied the opportunity to participate fully in family life. But it is women who are given lower pay, forced into poorer jobs, denied admission to schools, and excluded from other opportunities. Though it is by no means the only issue, the principal thrust of many women's rights groups is toward equal employment opportunity and a fairer share of the American economic pie, and most of the following projects deal with discriminatory job practices.

The most important piece of federal legislation in this regard is Title VII of the Civil Rights Act of 1964, which provides a strong guarantee of equal employment. Two features of Title VII are of particular benefit to citizen activists. The first is that the 1964 Civil Rights Act created the Equal Employment Opportunity Commission (EEOC) which stands ready to aid citizens bringing Title VII suits. Aid may consist of advice, intervention as a party in the case, or legal assistance in the form of an *amicus* brief, a supplementary brief submitted to the court by a party not directly involved in the litigation to support or oppose one of the contesting parties. To bring the EEOC into a case, a person who feels she suffered discrimination can fill out a simple one-page charge form briefly stating the facts of the case. Charge forms are available from EEOC local offices (check in phone directory under U.S. government), or by mail from the EEOC, Office of Public Information, 1500 G Street N.W., Washington, D.C. 20506. Once the charge form is filed, the EEOC is involved in the case, although because of a tremendous backlog of similar complaints, forthcoming action may be exceedingly slow.

The second important feature of Title VII is that it provides for payment of attorney's fees and court costs. In other words, the successful *litigant can recover the costs of litigation*. Even a person who has virtually no money may be able to hire a lawyer if her case is strong enough, since a victory pays court expenses and the attorney's fee. But cases drag on, and court costs are high; it may be difficult to find a lawyer willing to incur heavy costs, gambling on a victory reimbursement.

A further guarantee of equal employment is Executive Order 11246, as amended by Executive Order 11375. These orders specifically forbid all federal contractors from practicing employment discrimination. Contractors with outstanding government contracts in excess of $50,000 have an additional duty: they must carry out an affirmative action plan to seek out and employ women and members of minority groups at all levels of their company's operations.

There are a number of ways citizens can attack the problem of discrimination in employment. First, however, it is necessary to become familiar with its scope and pervasiveness. Women, for instance, constitute 38 percent of all fully employed workers in the United States. Yet the average working woman earns several thousand dollars a year less than the average working man. This discrimination cuts across racial lines. The Census Bureau reports that in 1970 the median wages for white and nonwhite males stood at $9,373 and $6,598 respectively, while the figures for white and nonwhite females were $5,490 and $4,674. Even within the same job category, women's incomes tend to be substantially lower than those of men. Evidence of employment discrimination can be found everywhere. A good example is as near as the telephone: the Bell System is the largest discriminator in the country. (In 1972 the Equal Employment Opportunity Commission issued a 20,000-page report detailing extensive racial, sexual, and national origin discrimination at AT&T; and when was the last time you got a male operator?) A glance at the "Help Wanted" column in almost any newspaper shows jobs open only to men or only to women. Men may have trouble recognizing a systematic pattern of sex discrimination, but women who have pounded the pavement looking for work only to find that they are unqualified on grounds of sex recognize it instantly.*

Once sensitized to the issue, projects can be developed to root out and eliminate discriminatory employment practices. A good place to start is where many jobs begin—at the employment agency or with ads in the "Help Wanted" columns of the newspaper.

How to Investigate Discrimination by Employment Agencies

Title VII of the Civil Rights Act applies not only to employers but to unions and employment agencies as well. There is an easy way to find out if employment agencies are acting in compliance with the law. Two job applicants, one male, one female (or, if race discrimination is suspected, one black, one white), should approach a series of agencies. They should be evenly matched academically and have the same work experience and career aims. In short, they should be as closely identical as possible in every way except sex

* The Rights of Women by Susan Ross (Avon Books, 1973) details various discriminatory practices against women and the legal remedies available to them.

(or race). The positions offered to each will demonstrate whether or not the agency is guilty of discrimination.

MPIRG, the Minnesota Public Interest Research Group, conducted several different studies of employment agencies in Minneapolis. In one telephone survey, a male and a female called 29 agencies in order to determine their referral policies. The personal data, such as age, education, backgrounds, experience, and interests were identical for both the male and female. The only difference was the sex of the caller.

The results were conclusive. In 96 percent of the calls clerical positions were discussed with the woman caller, compared to 10 percent who mentioned clerical to the male. Even here there was a difference. With the male they often added "of course, there's lots of room for advancement." Fifty-eight percent of the agencies told the woman that only clerical positions were open to her; none told that to the male caller. Often the woman and man caller were told, "Just a second, I'll have to connect you with someone who handles women's jobs" or "I'll connect you with someone who handles men's jobs"; sometimes the woman caller was told, "I'll connect you with the counselor who handles clerical jobs." Thus the structure of the agencies makes sexual discrimination inevitable.

One test alone is not conclusive. The MPIRG task force followed up the phone survey with field interviews. Again a male and female with identical credentials visited agencies on separate days looking for a "job with a good future." Again the results indicated a pattern of discrimination. Of the twenty-two interviews conducted by both men and women, 100 percent mentioned clerical work to the woman, compared to 1 percent who mentioned it to the man. Ninety-five percent of the agencies told the woman that the *only* area she would be able to get into was the clerical field; the man was never told that his only option was clerical work. The woman was often asked about children, marriage plans, etc., while the man never had to answer this type of question.

After concluding the survey, MPIRG issued a comprehensive report (available for $1.00) and promised to re-survey the agencies within a year.

This project can be duplicated in every city where there are employment agencies. To nail down the case, citizen activists might send in two or three crews of job applicants to the agency. If court action is contemplated, some of the applicants must be people actually looking for a job. This requirement is also necessary to file EEOC charges.

Careful notes should be taken of comments made by agency personnel, and a record should be kept of each opening to which the applicant was referred. If discrimination is uncovered, this information should be compiled in a report together with the résumés of the applicants and tables comparing the jobs and salaries offered to each. If publicity is desired, the information should be released to the press. If names and addresses of the agencies are provided, it will usually create a stir. The report should also be sent to the Equal Employment Opportunity Commission and to any local or state agency dealing with employment discrimination. There are also grounds for private legal action under Title VII, and attorneys in the area should be contacted about instituting a suit.

If the employment agencies voluntarily agree or are forced by court or EEOC action to cease discriminating, a follow-up study by different matched teams can monitor their progress and help to insure that bad habits don't return.

How to Investigate Employment Discrimination in Newspapers

In many parts of the country "Help Wanted" columns are still divided on the basis of sex: "Help Wanted Male" or "Help Wanted Female." This practice is blatantly discriminatory since it severely limits the choice of jobs available. Even though Title VII apparently doesn't apply to newspapers, many state and local laws do; women have used these laws successfully to force *The New York Times* and the *Pittsburgh Press* to cease discriminatory advertising.

Citizens can work to eliminate this type of discrimination in several ways. As a start, it is worth contacting the newspaper publisher and pointing out the harmful effects of sex-segregated advertising. Since a switch to plain "Help Wanted" columns won't cost the publisher money, he may be willing to accede to a request to do away with segregated columns voluntarily. If not, citizens should contact the city or state human rights or fair employment agency. As noted, some local laws specifically forbid this type of advertising. Others make it illegal for anyone to "aid or abet" a company to discriminate. At the very least a newspaper "aids and abets" when it places ads in sex-segregated columns. In either case, local authorities have the power to end this practice.

If there is no local or state law covering this form of discrimination, charges should be filed with the EEOC against the newspaper and against companies and agencies placing advertisements in sex-segregated columns. The applicability of Title VII to newspapers is in doubt, but the law certainly covers all companies and employment agencies. Since the law is clear, offending advertisers may pressure the newspaper to eliminate separate sex advertising or cease advertising altogether. This type of economic pressure may persuade a recalcitrant publisher to drop discriminatory columns.

If filing EEOC charges doesn't end this practice citizens can record the names of all companies or agencies using sex-segregated columns over a one-to-three-week period and file suit against them. A court can order them to cease advertising in a sex discriminatory fashion. Once all advertisers are forbidden to place ads in sex-segregated columns, the newspaper either will be forced to desegregate its columns or stop accepting advertising altogether, an alternative few papers can afford to accept. Thus, by use of this backdoor tactic, creative citizen activists can force newspapers to abandon this discriminatory practice against women.

How to Discover and Eliminate Sex Discriminatory State Labor Laws

Sometimes companies claim that they cannot hire women for certain jobs because state law forbids it. Many state labor laws do place limits on the number of hours women may work, the amount of weight they can lift, the conditions under which they can work, and in some cases, even forbid them to work at night. Such laws prevent women from working at jobs which they might prefer because of higher pay rates, better working conditions, or more prestige. Often their effect is to preserve overtime pay rates for men only. Working to eliminate these laws is a suitable project for individual or collective citizen action. In some states these laws have already been struck down as a violation of Title VII. There are many states, however, which still have such laws, so there is a continuing need for new legal actions.

The first step in this project is to look through state statutes to determine whether such laws are on the books. (A person does not have to be a lawyer to read statutes. All that is required is patience and a tolerance for jargon). Copies of the statutes can be found in most large public and university libraries, law offices, and city or town council offices. Usually, the first or last volume of statutes is an index which will indicate which sections cover the state labor law. A careful reading of these sections should reveal the extent of statutory discrimination against women workers.

Sometimes a simple call to the State Department of Labor will uncover the same information plus data on which of the laws are still being enforced. If a discriminatory law exists, the second step is to locate female workers willing to challenge it. They can be found through labor unions or women's groups in contact with working women. Since many state labor laws that discriminate against women have already been declared invalid, it may be easy to persuade companies to ignore them and state labor departments to cease enforcing them. If this doesn't work, it may be necessary to bring suit to invalidate the state labor law on the ground that it discriminates against women in violation of Title VII of the Civil Rights Act of 1964. Alternatively, since legal action may be costly, a citizens group might attempt to have the legislature amend these laws to bring them into conformity with Title VII.

The same goal will be accomplished if the Equal Rights Amendment to the federal Constitution is ratified by thirty-eight states. Helping secure ratification of this amendment is a project that should have the highest priority among the advocates of women's rights. Thirty-five state legislatures have considered the amendment already, and although most have passed it, a few have rejected it. After the long fight to secure congressional approval, it would be tragic if not enough support were mustered on the state level to ensure final passage. Citizens interested in working on this project should write to National Federation of Business and Professional Women's Clubs, 2012 Massachusetts Avenue, N.W., Washington, D.C. 20036; or Ann Scott, National Organization for Women, 1522 West Mount Royal, Baltimore, Maryland 27201. Either group will put them in contact with groups already working in their state.

How to Discover and Eliminate Job Segregation

Even when hiring is free of open discrimination, jobs may still be apportioned along sexual lines. The obvious example is the common practice of hiring only women for secretarial and clerical work, and only white males for skilled craft work. In addition to such longstanding practices, union contracts often establish job categories by sex, even though this practice is absolutely illegal. This type of job segregation is not usually obvious to the casual investigator. Even where it is noticed, people often accept job segregation subconsciously and are therefore unaware that it is illegal.

The same tactics used to eliminate discriminatory labor laws can be employed to wipe out job segregation. First, data have to be collected to prove that a pattern of discrimination exists. This data can be explicit, such as affidavits by women who are told that only certain jobs are open to them. It can be statistical, such as a survey revealing that 96 percent of all clerical jobs in a company are held by women and, correspondingly, that 94 percent of all managerial positions are occupied by men. The evidence can be even more compelling when jobs in similar capacities are rigidly segregated along sex lines as in hospitals when women are called nurse's aides and men orderlies even though they do the same work. Often the only real difference betwen jobs is the title, the sex of the job holder, and the lower pay scale for women. Besides explicit or statistical data, job segregation can sometimes be deduced from written job descriptions. Suddenly, in a description of jobs, the language changes from the general male words "he," "him," and "his" to "she," "her," "hers." This usually signals a segregated job categorization. Once job segregation has been documented, a Title VII action can be brought, or since the law is clear, an effort can be made to have the practice ended voluntarily. If unions are involved and are sympathetic, sex discrimination can become an issue for contract negotiation.

The preceding projects have all stressed court action as a means of eliminating discrimination. It is well to repeat again the unique provision of Title VII that makes an appeal to the courts possible, even though, ordinarily, citizens are kept out of court because of high litigation costs. Title VII provides for the successful complainant to recover the complete costs of attorneys fees plus other litigation disbursements.

Legal action is not the only way to end discrimination. The remaining projects in this section do not require an appeal to the courts.

How to Prevent Federal Contractors from Discriminating

Executive Order 11246, as amended by Executive Order 11375, prohibits all federal contractors from practicing employment discrimination on grounds of race or sex. It is difficult for the average citizen to investigate and prove discrimination against the largest federal contractors, which employ thousands of workers in plants scattered throughout the country. But there are other contractors, which are more localized, more open to investigation, and far more susceptible to citizen action. Virtually all colleges and universities, for instance, have some contracts with the federal government. Contracts in excess of $10,000 can be canceled if a pattern of discrimination in employment is found to exist.

A study of the positions held by women at most universities reveals a pattern of blatant discrimination. Starting with the number of bachelor degrees granted to women and proceeding up to Ph.D.s, there is a steady decline in the number of female students. (There is also a decline in the percentage of applicants who are women. This fact is not necessarily a valid defense, however, since the decline in the number of female applicants may reflect discrimination: people don't apply for positions they think they will not get.) The same pattern is found among the faculty. Women frequently reach the instructor level, and a few become associate professors. But very few become full professors and almost none become department heads or deans—except in "specialized" fields, such as nursing or home economics. Professional schools are often the worst offenders in this regard. Even more obvious is the discrimination in the division between largely female clerical staffs and male craft workers in the university.

The existence of these patterns of discrimination may be proved simply by analyzing the school catalogue. Tables can be drawn which clearly chart the topography of a school's discrimination. Interviews with outspoken faculty members can add personal experiences to give life to the statistics. These can be compiled into a report which should be turned over to the Department of Health, Education, and Welfare (HEW), school and local newspapers, and broadcast media. It should also be sent to state and federal representatives and senators, and to the local human rights commission. If the school does not immediately begin a program to wipe out discrimination, stronger action may be required. While the courts stand as a last resort if discrimination is found in public undergraduate, graduate, vocational, or professional schools (private undergraduate schools are not covered), sufficient pressure can often be brought by aroused students and faculty to end this type of discrimination.

A slightly different situation exists in the case of major contractors. Many large universities fall into this category because they have federal contracts in excess of $50,000. Contractors in this category have a special duty: as a condition of their contract, they must submit and abide by an "affirmative action plan." An affirmative action plan requires prospective contractors to submit to the federal government an exact plan for increasing the number of women and minorities in the company's employ and for promoting those already employed. In other words, not only is the contractor bound not to discriminate, he is pledged actively to recruit new employees who previously may have suffered because of discrimination. The range of action required under affirmative action is extremely broad. The theory behind affirmative action is that without positive effort the accumulated weight of years of active discrimination will defeat any strictly evenhanded policy. Since most qualified women and minorities *believe* they cannot get certain jobs, whether or not this belief is justified, they will not bother to apply. The affirmative action plan places a burden on the contractor to seek women out, to convince them to apply, and then to hire them.

Affirmative action plans are matters of public information. Their effects can be precisely measured since they require the contractor to state specific employment goals. Citizen investigators can compare before-and-after employment figures to determine the company's progress. If none is being made and if patterns of discrimination are revealed, a report should be sent to the Department of Health, Education, and Welfare with a request to freeze all government monies until the terms of the contract are complied with. However, it should be noted that HEW has in the past been reluctant to take action, and unless considerable pressure can be brought, is unlikely to adopt a vigorous posture in the future.

How to Eliminate Sex Discrimination in Public Schools

The Citizens Advisory Council on the Status of Women recently called on citizens interested in education to conduct a review of their local public school system to measure the degree of sex discrimination present. The council charged that

systematic surveys of public schools in Ann Arbor, Michigan, and New York City by women's organizations document areas of inferiority in the educational opportunities afforded girls in all levels of the public schools surveyed. The Council believes that similar conditions are common in the many public school systems throughout the country.*

The council pointed out six areas where discrimination is likely to be present:
—Single-sex public schools.
—Courses in coeducational schools restricted to one sex.
—Expenditure, for physical education courses and extra-curricular activities.
—Textbooks, library books and other curriculum aids (see next project).

* A copy of the Council's memorandum is available from The Citizens Advisory Council on the Status of Women, Room 1336, Department of Labor Building, Washington, D.C. 20210.

—School activities such as hall patrols, safety squads, room chores, etc.

—Promotion of teachers.

Citizens interested in working to eliminate sex discrimination in schools should make contact with PTA chapters, teachers' organizations, and local women's groups. The first step is to make a preliminary survey of the local public school system to determine where problems lie. The New York City survey found that in 1971, twelve public schools were open to boys only, but only five were exclusively for girls. Two of the best schools in the city, Stuyvesant High School of Science and Mathematics and Brooklyn Technical High School, were opened to girls in 1969 as the result of court action, but are grossly imbalanced. By 1971 there were still only 446 girls in a student body of 2,322 at Stuyvesant and 180 girls in a student body of 5,000 at Brooklyn Technical.

Sex-segregated courses are more common than single-sex schools but they are harder to discover. Shop, sewing, and cooking classes are good areas to examine first. School course descriptions should be surveyed and guidance counselors should be questioned to discover whether bias is revealed. For example, if cooking and sewing course descriptions use female pronouns, like "she," "her," "hers," while physics, chemistry, and shop courses use "he," "him," or "his," a climate of discrimination is created. A more conclusive test would be to see if guidance counselors ever refer boys to home economics courses or girls to shop. A follow-up investigation might study whether teachers in these courses discriminate against members of one sex.

Athletics and physical education courses are activities where discrimination is most common. Per capita expenditures on these activities by sex are an objective measure of this discrimination. Another measure is the number of hours per week facilities are open to boys compared to the time available to girls. Girls seldom have equal use of tennis or basektball courts, swimming pools, or gymnasiums. The number of coaches supplied to boys' teams in contrast to girls' teams is another standard that can be used to test whether discrimination is present.

Female teachers often are limited in their opportunities for promotion. Not only are female teachers themselves harmed by discriminatory practices, but girl students are also denied the opportunity to see women exercising important roles. This pattern of employment discrimination was charted by the National Education Association (NEA) and was reported in the association's *Research Bulletin* 49, October, 1971, in an article entitled "Professional Women in Public Schools 1970–71." According to the NEA

women constitute 84.7 percent of elementary school teachers but only 19.4 percent of supervisory principals, and 30.2 percent of teaching principals (usually in smaller schools); 45.9 percent of secondary teachers, but 35.3 percent of junior high principals, and 3.0 percent of high school principals.

Once the citizens group has surveyed the school system and documented areas of discrimination, a meeting should be arranged with the Board of Education at which a report of the survey's findings should be presented. Representatives of other citizens organizations should be invited to participate in the presentation. Some resistance should be expected; stereotypes are hard to break down. But if the evidence is clear and the citizens group has community support, the board may voluntarily agree to end discrimination. If it does, an action plan with an explicit timetable can be drawn up, publicly agreed upon and then printed in local papers as evidence of the board's resolution.

If the board is unwilling to act, there are other avenues open to resourceful activists. The state Board of Education may have power to order local boards to cease discriminating. Or there may be a state law or an equal rights provision in the state constitution preventing discrimination. Illinois, Pennsylvania, and Virginia, for example, have equal rights provisions in their state constitutions.

Another way to bring about equality is by persuading HEW to enforce Title IX of Public Law 92-318, the education amendments of the 1972 act. It provides that "no person in the United States shall, on the basis of sex, be excluded from participation in, be denied benefits of, or be subjected to discrimination under any education program or activity receiving Federal financial assistance." Complaints should be sent to Office of Education, Department of Health, Education, and Welfare, 400 Maryland Avenue S.W., Washington, D.C. 20201. Copies of the complaint should be sent to the state's senatory and the representative for the district in which the school is located.

Citizen activists can also attempt to make sex discrimination an issue in the selection of Board of Education members. All candidates for the school board should be urged to take a stand on the question of equal treatment for women.

How to Improve the Image
of Women in Textbooks

One reason that many women do not aspire to careers as doctors, lawyers, airplane pilots, or scientists is that the image they have of themselves denies them these roles. A person's self-image comes from many sources—family, friends, the media, and school. One important source is the image a child sees portrayed in school textbooks. A casual survey of these textbooks, especially readers and social studies texts, reveals a massive pattern of discrimination against women. A more detailed study only intensifies the original impression. Women, as a rule, appear far less frequently in these books than do men. When they do, they are usually portrayed as weak, dependent, passive, and domestic creatures, having few activities of their own.

A report by the National Organization for Women* on readers used in New York City public schools found that

in the early grade readers the oldest child in a family is always a boy. Boys are associated with making, earning, playing active games, learning, romping with dogs and helping their fathers. Girls are associated with helping their mothers or brothers, playing with kittens, getting into minor forms of trouble and being helped out by their brothers. Patterns of dependence, passivity and domesticity are apparent. Story lines from Scott Foreman's first three primers go as follows:

> Boys set up carnival act. Boy teaches dog to jump for food. Boy solves problem of keeping mother's floors clean. Boy solves problem of runaway dog. Boy plays ball. Boy uses magnet to solve problem for girl. Boy builds car, girls interfere.

Story lines for girls go:

> Girl is frightened by older brother. Girl is helped by older brother. Girls play with Teddy and kitten. Girl is helped by older boy. Girls solve their own problem (this is very unusual). Girl mistakes cat on television for her own kitten. Girl goes shopping with mother. Girl helps mother choose books. Girl paints picture of cat.

In most texts, the woman executive, the police heroine, the female cab driver, or the woman doctor are nowhere to be found. The lack of strong, resourceful female images is inevitably absorbed by impressionable children and helps to perpetuate a role model destructive for both sexes, but especially for women.

Citizens can do a great deal to change the prevailing image of women. In the early 1960s, civil rights activists did much to eliminate the "Sambo" image from school books. The same effort can be made for women. Schools plead that no textbooks are without sex discrimination and, in many cases, they are correct. However, some books are better than others, and if citizens begin to pressure strongly enough for

---

* *Report on Sex Bias in the Public Schools*, National Organization for Women, New York Chapter, 28 East 56th Street, New York, New York 10022, $2.25.

change the school will force publishers to issue new materials. A forty-eight-page bibliography of books which do not discriminate entitled *Little Miss Muffitt Fights Back* can be obtained for $0.40 from Feminists on Children's Media, Box 4315, Grand Central Station, New York, New York 10017.

How to Improve the Image and Employment Opportunities of Women in Radio and Television

IMAGE

All television and radio stations broadcast on public airwaves. In order to use these public properties, they must meet certain qualifications. Their success is checked every three years when radio and television stations must renew their broadcast licenses. Stations in one-third of the states renew their licenses each year. The schedule of renewal dates can be obtained free by writing to the Federal Communications Commission, 1919 M Street N.W., Washington, D.C. 20036. To learn more about the qualifications that stations must meet and about the duty of stations to "serve the public interest," read *Guide to Citizen Action in Radio and T.V.*, by Marsha O'Bannion Prowitt, available from Office of Communications, United Church of Christ, 289 Park Avenue South, New York, New York 10010.

For those interested in eliminating sex discrimination and improving the image of women in the media, the avenues for citizen action are numerous. An initial project would be to determine how frequently and in what roles women appear on television. The question of "frequency" is a quantitative study; the question of "roles" is qualitative. Accurate answers to these questions require several weeks of dawn-to-midnight monitoring of all programs appearing on the station under observation.

Such studies have been undertaken by women's groups in New York City and Washington, D.C. Both discovered the same pattern repeating itself. Women appear on television far less frequently than men and, when they are on screen, often portray weak, helpless, ignorant creatures more prized for their bodies than for their brains. The women's groups have brought an action before the Federal Communications Commission (FCC) to deny station WABC-TV in New York and WRC-TV in Washington their license renewals.

The methodology of the study is simple. Standard forms should be prepared with space to list the number of women or minorities that appear and what characters they portray. Special attention should be given to newscasts to determine what portion of the news is devoted to women's news, such as abortion reform efforts or attempts to ratify the equal rights amendment. Even allowing for the disparity in numbers between male and female newsmakers, women's news is underreported, many women contend. A close monitoring and analysis will help indicate whether this is the case.

Commercials should also be analyzed. The New York and Washington petitions to deny license renewals charged that commercials reinforced discriminatory stereotypes of women and men. By airing the commercials, the stations in effect were presenting only one side of an important issue (women's role) and thus were violating the fairness doctrine. The FCC has not yet ruled on this contention.

At the end of the monitoring period, one must prepare a report incorporating all of the data that has been gathered, the conclusions arising from it, and the names of the monitors. The report should be forwarded to the FCC. The FCC is required to include every report, letter, or even comments on postcards in the station's file and to consider them at renewal time.

A continuing study of discrimination in broadcasting with extensive local publicity, even if insufficient to prevent license renewal, may pressure stations into voluntary compliance with equal media opportunity. Already most major stations have a few token women, blacks, or other minorities. Continued pressure can help expand this representation to make equality of the airwaves a reality.

EMPLOYMENT

The Federal Communications Commission is concerned with more than on-screen appearances of women and minorities. The commission recently adopted rules which require all stations to develop "positive recruitment, training, job design and other measures in order to ensure genuine equality of opportunities to participate fully in all organizational units, occupations and levels of responsibility in the station." This means that women must be hired to perform more than secretarial functions and that women, blacks, and other minorities must be sought after—actively recruited—to fill positions at all levels of responsibility within the station. A station cannot point to a full quota of women secretaries and black janitors as evidence of its affirmative policies. Each station must file with the FCC an annual report on May 31 detailing statistics on station recruitment and employment of "Blacks, Orientals, American Indians, Spanish-surnamed Americans and Women"; the report is open to public inspection at the station during regular business hours.

In November, 1972, the United Church of Christ issued an analysis of the employment practices of 609 television stations.* The report showed that only 22 percent of the 39,071 full-time employees were women and that 75 percent of these were engaged in office and clerical jobs. Over half the stations had no women in management. The report concluded that "many stations show little or no response to the FCC-mandated priority of providing equal employment opportunities. Some have actually reduced the proportion of their staffs which are drawn from minority group members and women."

At present, the FCC does not have the resources to investigate closely every radio and television station's practices. Generally, an uncontested license application receives only cursory attention and renewal is automatic. But a strong citizen challenge based on data and statistics compiled by monitors or through investigations of the station's annual reports is bound to be considered carefully. What's more, if the FCC proves responsive to citizen efforts, a deterrence factor will be created that will tend to move stations towards voluntary compliance with these standards.

There are numerous other projects which citizens individually or collectively can undertake to better the status of women. Using techniques described elsewhere in this book, citizens can promote more and better daycare centers, thus freeing more women to seek employment outside the home; they can lobby for new laws to extend women's rights or to repeal discriminatory provisions in existing laws; they can protest with letters, counter-ads, or boycotts against advertisers who exploit women by portraying them as beautiful but brainless creatures. In other ways as well, personally and publicly, citizen groups can seek to give to women (and minorities) the full status of equal citizenship.

* *Television Station Employment Practices: The Status of Minorities and Women,* by Ralph M. Jennings.

IV

SHIFTING THE TAX BURDEN

Property taxes account for about 85 percent of locally raised revenue. This means that the adequacy of schools, sanitation, police, health, and other services provided by local government depends in large measure upon property tax. Unfortunately, much of the available evidence points to poor administration of this tax. Often assessors, who carry out day-to-day administrative duties, are untrained, underpaid, and have too few assistants. Worse, many have serious economic and political conflicts of interest. Tax laws themselves are riddled with loopholes and exemptions which enable the privileged and powerful to evade payment, while burdening other citizens with a disproportionately large payment.

Field investigations repeatedly have demonstrated the truth of these statements:

—Common Cause in Denver, Colorado found that while homes were assessed at 23 percent of fair market value, major businesses were assessed at much less—as low as 4 percent and even 1 percent of fair market value.

—The John C. Lincoln Institute of Hartford, Connecticut, found that mainly low-income, black districts of Hartford were assessed at over 60 percent of full market value, while middle- and upper-income neighborhoods were being assessed at under 50 percent.

—The Citizens Action Project of Chicago, Illinois, found that two entire residential neighborhoods were assessed 25 percent higher than what the assessor said the average assessment ratio was.

—Professors Oliver Oldman and Henry Aaron of Harvard University found that assessments in a poor, black neighborhood of Boston were about 75 percent of full market value, while in a wealthier white neighborhood they were less than half that high.

The three projects in this section show you how to investigate property taxes in your own community. Two deal with industrial and corporate assessments. The final project lists ways the homeowner can check his own assessment. This chapter is organized differently from the rest. Because the solution to any problem uncovered in the research is essentially the same for all projects, it is put last and the various research techniques are described first.

Industrial Assessment: How to Estimate Whether Industry Is Paying Its Property Taxes

Do major industries pay their fair share of property taxes? Many taxpayers would like to know the answer to this question, and the following project gives them six ways to check the property tax assessments of large industrial plants.

These methods yield only rough estimates, but they can sometimes be surprisingly accurate; they are certainly enough to alert a citizen to substantial underassessments. And that's all that is needed. Besides, even the most thorough and "scientific" assessment is itself only an approximation.

Citizens should take account of special laws and regulations regarding depreciation, pollution-control devices, and the breakdown between real and personal property. At the same time, they should be alert to official "regulations" that are really illegal giveaways. The help of experienced professionals—such as realtors, contractors, appraisers, and attorneys—should be sought whenever possible. On the other hand, don't underestimate what a resourceful amateur can do.

Expert Opinion. A Ralph Nader study group needed a rough idea of what Union Camp's paper bag plant in Savannah, Georgia, was worth. To get an initial estimate they simply asked officials at other paper companies. The estimates they received, ranging from $375 million to $550 million, strongly suggested that the $90 million on which Union Camp was paying taxes was much too low. Additional evidence gathered more scientifically tended to confirm these estimates.

Employment–Capital Ratio. Since U.S. Steel in Gary, Indiana, won't open its books to the assessor—or even to the mayor—city officials have had to use their wits. Gary's finance advisor, Arnold Rhinegold, used the following method, according to the *Wall Street Journal* of April 5, 1971. Rhinegold found that 14 percent of all U.S. Steel's employees were in Gary. Assuming the ratio of employees to taxable assets there to be average, he reasoned that 14 percent of the company's property should be in Gary, too. He found the value of all the company's property from an annual report and took 14 percent. The result showed that U.S. Steel's Gary assessment was at least $110 million too low. Even this method can be conservatively valued. A company may carry assets like land on its balance sheets at their original purchase price, even though the market value today is much more. And machinery and equipment may be worth much more than the depreciated value on the company's books.

Output–Capital Ratio. The Citizen Action Project (CAP) in Chicago used a method similar to Mr. Rhinegold's to check the assessment on U.S. Steel's South Works there. But CAP based its estimate on the plant's output instead of on the number of people employed there. Using information from annual reports and other company publications, CAP was able to find that South Works produced 11.5 percent of U.S. Steel's total raw steel output. It found further that 80 percent of the company's revenue came from steel production and fabrication. Therefore, the CAP researchers reasoned, about 80 percent of the company's property was probably used to produce steel, and about 11.5 percent of that was probably at the South Works. CAP was careful to exclude pollution-control equipment—tax free under state law—and to estimate the assessor's depreciation formula (since he wouldn't disclose it), then to apply it to their figures. CAP calculated a value of $195.3 million—a bit more than the $45.7 million on the assessment rolls!

Rules of Thumb. Insurance companies and investment advisors have "rules of thumb" for estimating the value of different kinds of property. Any property which falls into a specific category (i.e., 200-ton-per-day pulp mill) is assessed at a certain rate. Current figures for steel mills, for example, are said to range from $300 to $350 per ton of annual output. Try to get the figure for the type of industry you are looking at. The "rule-of-thumb" approach makes a good check on a more complicated method. And it can stand alone if necessary.

Corporate Braggadocio. Corporations often vaunt to the press the value of new plants and equipment. And they like to impress stockholders and potential investors with such figures in annual reports. But their arithmetic is not always the same when the tax assessor comes to call. During the 1960s, the Sara Lee Baking Company built an ultramodern, mechanized bakery in Deerfield, Illinois, a suburb of Chicago. A local attorney read in company advertisements and in a national magazine article that the plant cost $22 million. Yet he found it on the assessment rolls at only $4.5 million ($5.25 million minus about .7 million for "personal property"), or 20 percent of what the company said was full value. The attorney's own home was assessed at 55 percent of full value!

If a company doesn't build a whole new plant but merely installs new equipment or makes additions, find out what these improvements were and how much they cost (see next paragraph). Then compare these amounts with the change in the company's property tax assessment during that period.

Other Sources of Information. Use imagination! Where might records of property values appear? And where might a citizen get costs of different kinds of equipment and facilities?

Of course sales prices, as recorded on deeds or reported in newspapers, would be the best guide. However, large industrial plants are not often bought or sold. But how about building permits? Or catalogues of equipment manufacturers? Or studies prepared for labor wage negotiations (if available)?

State utility commissions have records of the property values of railroads, power utilities, and so forth. The Federal Power Commission and the Atomic Energy Commission also may have useful information. Companies may have to file information on property values for licenses or permits. Court records may be helpful: has the company recently been involved in a contested merger or acquisition? Annual reports, the Securities and Exchange Commission, and state securities commissions are other possible sources.

The local assessor may or may not be helpful. Learn as much from him as you can regarding the company's assessment and exactly how he reached it. And find out how much a citizen is entitled by law to see.

Another source of information is the company itself. A carefully worded letter to the company president asking for specific information may receive a helpful reply. Anyway, nothing is lost by trying.

In general, it is a good idea to use several of these methods and sources at the same time, as a check on one another. Err on the side of conservatism. Take into account as many special laws and circumstances as can be found. And remember it is only a rough estimate, not a professional appraisal.

How to Discover Corporate Tax Dodges

Underassessment is not the only way that large commercial and industrial taxpayers avoid paying their fair share of property taxes. It is just one of their many tax avoidance tricks. Some are blatantly illegal; others have been graced with the mantle of the "law." But they all have one thing in common: by cutting taxes on large property interests they make small local taxpayers pay more.

I. ILLEGAL TAX AVOIDANCE

Nonlisting

Few taxpayers realize that much taxable property never even gets onto the tax rolls. Improvements or additions to existing structures, new commercial and industrial equipment, business inventories, and "intangibles" (where they are taxed) are prime example; but entire buildings and even land sometimes mysteriously stay off the tax rolls. Either the assessor is so slipshod that he lacks a system for getting new property onto the rolls, or he is simply shutting his eyes. Assessors sometimes give developers a free ride by waiting until a homebuyer buys a newly built home to assess it. A careful check of the assessment roll in your community will reveal such untaxed property. Try checking the assessment roll against building permits, for example, to see whether the assessor has been winking at new construction.

Removing Property from the Jurisdiction

Incredible as it may sound, some businesses actually move their property out of a jurisdiction on assessment day just to avoid the property tax. Sometimes these maneuvers are illegal; at other times they are within the inadvertent loopholes of the law. But in either case they leave the small taxpayer holding the bag. How does it happen? Construction firms and strip miners move their equipment across county and even state lines. Businessmen load their inventories onto boxcars. Chicago bankers have a technique more befitting the Keystone Cops than the pillars of the community they deem themselves. They call it the "rollover"; on assessment day they transfer their taxable accounts to out-of-state banks, or they invest them in tax-free securities. A week or so later they sell the bonds and get their accounts back. Five major Chicago banks, including the First National and Continental Illinois, used the "rollover" to deprive Cook County of $3 million in property taxes in 1970. Such tax-cheaters are greatly assisted by property tax laws that fix assessments as of one particular day, instead of figuring them on the average value the taxpayer had during the year.

There are more subtle forms of this ploy. Business firms will arrange their purchases so that their inventories are at low ebb on assessment day; a few days later a huge shipment will arrive. Firms sometimes trick the assessor by buying equipment through out-of-state subsidiaries. The subsidiary pays the regular price, then turns around and "sells" the goods to the in-state firm for much less. The in-state firm shows the assessor the bill of sale, and the phony price becomes its assessment losses. Or firms will avoid the property tax entirely by "leasing" equipment instead of buying it. Suppose State A allows very low assessments on, or exempts entirely, a certain kind of business property—such as railroad boxcars. And suppose the company wants to operate in State B, which taxes these more heavily. Our businessman will set up a subsidiary in State A to buy the equipment and then "lease" it to the operation in State B. Meanwhile, homeowners are voting down school budgets because their property taxes are too high.

Too Much Depreciation

Assessors usually allow "depreciation" on commercial and industrial property; that is, they reduce its assessment each year because supposedly it is wearing out. Fair enough—at least where the property is in fact going down in value. But "depreciation" covers a multitude of property tax sins. First, assessors sometimes reduce assessments on business property automatically, even though its value may have stayed the same or gone even higher. Second, assessors often allow too much depreciation. For example, they may let businessmen use the Internal Revenue Service depreciation rates, even though these bear no relation at all to the fair market value of the property and make its value seem much less than it actually is. In effect, then, the assessor uses depreciation as a way to give an obscure and illegal exemption to business taxpayers.

Here are some ways to ferret out excess depreciation:

—Ask the assessor for his depreciation formula for different kinds of property. Compare them to IRS formulas and to formulas given in handbooks for industrial appraisers, and to prices quoted in used-equipment catalogues (available, for example, from the Equipment Guide Book Co., Box 10113, Palo Alto, California 94303).

—Ask the state assessment agency for the depreciation

guidelines it issues to local assessors (if it does so). Does the assessor follow these? Are they themselves too generous?

—Compare the assessments on specific pieces of commercial and industrial equipment with prices quoted in used-equipment catalogues.

These are a few examples. Your imagination and determination may reveal other ways as well.

A final point on depreciation. Assessors often let commercial and industrial property owners overallocate their total property value to their buildings and improvements, and underallocate it to their land. In other words, if the property is worth $1,000 altogether—$500 for the land and $500 for the buildings and improvements—the assessor allows a breakdown of $250 for the land and $750 for the improvements. What is the difference? Plenty. The owner gets $250 extra to write off as depreciation (he can depreciate buildings and improvements but not land). This way he cheats not only other local property taxpayers but the Internal Revenue Service as well.

More on Assessment Cheating

Excess depreciation is just the beginning of assessment fudging. There are many ways assessors can whittle and shave a complex commercial or industrial assessment. In Virginia, a group of persistent taxpayers found the assessor had been allowing a "vacancy factor" on buildings that were leased solidly for years to come. In Chicago, the assessor cooked up his own device, a "condition factor," to soften the assessment on large commercial and industrial properties.

Inventing bogus assessment-reducers, or fudging on genuine ones, takes effort, and not all assessors bother. Some just sit down with the big taxpayer—and perhaps with local politicos and bigwigs as well—and "negotiate" the assessment. They may just let the corporate taxpayer write his own.

How to root out such doings? Hard questioning of the assessor, public officials both in and out of office, attorneys, and others close to the scene, may lay bare "negotiated" assessments. And if the assessor has little or no data to back up his assessment of a certain property, that in itself is a tip-off.

But to uncover cheating with the assessment formula, a citizen needs to bone up on assessment techniques or work with someone who already knows about them. The citizen must gain access to the assessor's records, pore over them, and demand explanations when the figures seem out of line. This is hard work, yet citizens have done it. And in the process they have done a service both to themselves and to their communities. For there is an important principle at stake here. Is the assessor to reign as high priest over a system so complicated and obscure that no one can tell whether or not it is fair?

If the assessor is open and honest—as many are—he will not feel threatened by citizen efforts, so long as they respect his own time and duties. Normally an assessor with nothing to hide will welcome the chance to gain the confidence of the public. But if he tries to avoid or obstruct citizen inquiries and to keep his doings a secret—take notice.*

Delinquency

Many taxpayers, business and nonbusiness, do not pay their taxes. Their number is surprisingly large. Some tax "delinquents" are simply people who don't have the money. But others are careful schemers. Tax delinquency can be very good business. Penalties for delinquency are often so light that even if the delinquent taxpayer is caught, he will merely have received, in effect, a low-interest loan from the local government—that is, from the local taxpayer. Often, however, because local governments are so short of man-

---

* He may, for example, be required by law to keep certain records confidential. In that case, the problem is with the law, not necessarily with him.

power, and enforcement procedures are so rickety, the delinquent may not be caught for years, if ever. Political influence of course plays a part in this kind of property tax malpractice as in others.

Find out from the local tax collector the total amount of unpaid taxes—delinquencies—for current and past years, and find out also who the delinquents are. Figure out how much extra all other taxpayers, including yourself, have had to pay in order to make up for these delinquents. Figure out how much they took from the local schools. Then go to the local prosecutor, or whatever official is responsible, and find out what action he has taken against the delinquents.

If a can of worms turns up, don't be surprised. There are plenty of them hidden within the property tax structure.

II. LEGALIZED TAX AVOIDANCE

Whereas petty thieves break the law, powerful special interests can often change the law to serve their greed. These interests have made the property tax law their special playground. And the whole subject is so obscure that small taxpayers often don't know what is going on. They lash out at school budgets when the real problem is in laws that make them pay more than their share. So understanding *how* the law serves private greed is the first step. That done, citizens will be ready to act effectively, through both the legislature and the courts, to change the law to serve justice instead.

Here are some of the common legal deals that strip the hide of small taxpayers.

Low-Tax Zones

"No man is an island," but commercial and industrial taxpayers sometimes are. They arrange for state or local officials to set up special low-tax zones around their plants. Or these officials will set up such industrial "tax havens" to bribe new industries to move into their jurisdictions.

In effect the special zone builds a legal wall between the businesses and the revenue needs of the communities around them. These communities have to serve the people who work in the plants. They must provide schools for the workers' children. They must suffer the congestion and pollution that the plants impose. But the businesses in the special zones pay little or nothing. They may even get free services like roads, fire and police protection, water, and sewers.

Of course there may be some taxes within the special district. But since there are few if any residents, and almost no school children, costs and hence taxes there will be very low. The free ride on taxes is not the only reason industries favor these low-tax zones. They also like the control the zones give them over local ordinances—such as possible ones against noise and pollution. Their racket and filth may carry over into surrounding communities, but people there can do nothing about it. The industry is safely behind a legal barricade—the low-tax zone.

Special Districts

There is an even more cunning way that private interests ride free on the backs of local property taxpayers—the "special district." These are units of local government set up to provide a particular service, such as sewers, irrigation, flood, or insect control. Some special districts may really serve the public. But others are mainly schemes for pumping property taxes into private hands.

Texas "water districts" illustrate the latter. In general, this is how they work: a developer will influence the right public officials to set up a "special water district" around land he wants to develop. He next moves a few people— perhaps employees or associates—into the district who thereby become "residents," though they may be living in trailers. These "residents" then "vote" for the special district to sell bonds to pay for improvements. The bond issues may be for millions of dollars; in one Houston, Texas, case six "residents" approved a bond issue of $24 million.

The developer then uses the proceeds to make improvements he himself would otherwise have to pay for. He also uses them to bestow handsome fees upon architecture, law, and engineering firms with whom he may be connected.

Of course, the people who later buy homes in the development and become bona fide residents inherit this debt, and have to pay it off through their property taxes. And the whole matter is so obscure that they may not even realize they are doing so.

Industrial Development Bonds

There is an even more blatant form of property tax charity for the private business interests—the "industrial development bond." When state and local governments borrow money by selling bonds, they rightfully do so only to build a facility for the public, like a hospital or a school. It is illegal to use public funds or credit to serve a private purpose. But with industrial development bonds, the public actually goes into debt to build a plant for a private business! The excuse is that the business provides jobs for local residents, and that it therefore serves a "public purpose." But by that standard the public should finance every local business venture.

The business gets a long-term lease to the plant the public has financed. Since the state or locality still owns the property, it is exempt: the business pays no property taxes.

Thus small local taxpayers not only have to pay off the bond issue that financed the company's plant, they have to pick up the industry's share of the local property tax as well. That includes the extra costs the plant itself imposes, such as police and fire protection, water and sewerage, pollution and congestion.

And not to be outdone, Uncle Sam has cooked up his

own part of the giveaway. The wealthy investors who buy these "industrial development bonds" and exact interest from the local taxpayers pay no federal income tax on the interest; the bonds are a form of "tax-free municipals."

There is something in it for everyone, in short, except for the small local taxpayer.

Exemptions

"Uniformity" was once the basis of the property tax—all taxpayers treated alike. But today the property tax laws are full of exemptions and favors for special interests. Home-owners who wonder why the property tax is becoming so heavy might well look at these.

Whole classes of property may be exempt, such as business inventories or equipment. Or an exemption may be a gift to one favored group. In 1968 California Governor Ronald Reagan signed into law a bill that in effect exempted films from the property tax.

There are ways to bestow exemptions through the back door so that the public does not see them. The assessment day for business inventories, for example, may be set at a time when these are very low. Depreciation is another way. The legislature or public officials may allow such rapid depreciation on business property that it all but disappears from the tax rolls.

Still another way that private businesses stay off the tax rolls is by leasing property owned by government agencies. Hotels, banks, and stores lease buildings and space from airport and port authorities; defense contractors lease plants from the Defense Department. If the state does not tax the so-called leasehold interest in these properties, then the businesses get a free ride on the government's exemption. (If such deals sound like the "industrial development bond" above, it is not by chance. They are just different ways to skin the same cat—the small taxpayer.)

Businesses contrive to hide behind exemptions not meant for them at all. For example, some states provide special low assessments for farmland and open spaces. These are supposed to ease the tax load on small farmers and help keep such lands out of development. But developers and speculators, including giants like Levitt and Boise Cascade, will buy low while they wait for the land to "ripen" (command top money for development). And they can usually beat down the state legislature efforts to make them pay back the property tax break they received.

Not all unjust exemptions go to private businesses, however. The "sacred cows" among property tax exemptions—like those for homeowners, veterans, the elderly, churches, and charities—usually go to all regardless of need. Millionaires as well as paupers benefit. Churches, charities, and other nonprofit bodies may be exempt on property they put to commercial uses, such as parking lots and office buildings. The injustice of this set-up is widely recognized. But few legislators dare to tamper with it. The public will have to lead if the sacred cows of property tax exemptions are to be undone.

Is Your Own Assessment Fair?

So far we've talked about other people's assessments and taxes, and how to tell whether they are fair. Now what about your *own* assessment? Is it fair? Or are you paying more than you should, in relation to others?

Let's try to clear up one point first. Just what do we mean by a "fair" assessment? We mean what the law says the assessment should be. (Whether or not you think the laws themselves need change, is an important matter but one which we cannot discuss here.) In almost every state, the law says that assessments should be at "full market value," or at some definite percentage of full market value.

"Full market value" simply means what a buyer would pay for the property. In some states the law uses different words, like "fair market value" or "full cash value." But the meaning is the same. It's how much someone who wanted to buy your property would pay for it.

The chances are that your assessment is nowhere near that much. Why? Because in many states the courts have given in to what the assessors were doing anyway and have said that assessment at full market value isn't all that important. What *is* important, these courts have said, is that assessments be *uniform*. And by "uniform," they mean that every property owner should be assessed at the same percentage of full market value. (Except in the few states which require a different percentage for different kinds of property.)

In theory this is fine. Because if everyone is indeed assessed at the same percentage of fair market value, then the portion of the total tax burden that each one bears stays the same. But in practice, these court rulings fall flat. With the "full market value" standard out the window, taxpayers have little or no idea how to judge their own assessment or the assessment of others. And studies have shown that the lower assessed values are to full market value (the "assessment-sales ratio"), the greater the inequities there are likely to be between taxpayers.

But that is for another day. For now, just remember that an assessment is "fair" if it is at the same percentage of fair market value as is everyone else's. Fine. How can you tell whether an assessment is or isn't?

Note first that there are, in the main, three ways you might be getting the short end of the stick. First, your own house or property might be overassessed in comparison to those of your neighbors. (Or, conversely, some individual might be getting a big break compared to yourself and everyone else.) Second, even though your own assessment may be on a par with those of your neighbors, your whole neighborhood may be overassessed in comparison with another neighborhood. And third, you yourself and all the other homeowners, or people who live in or have property like yours, may be overassessed in comparison to people who hold some other type of property.

Let's deal with these one at a time.

COMPARING YOUR OWN ASSESSMENT TO THOSE OF YOUR NEIGHBORS

How do you compare your own assessment with those of your neighbors? The easiest way is to pick out the houses in your neighborhood that are most like your own. Then go to the assessor's office and find out what their assessments are. If there are large differences, ask the assessor why. If he doesn't have a good answer, then it's time to act.

A better way is to compare assessments to sales prices, because these are the best index of what full market value really is. In this method, you don't have to worry so much whether the other homes or properties are exactly like your own. Because the *ratio* of assessment to sales price should be the same regardless.

First you need to find the "assessment-sales ratio" on your own property. If you bought it recently, this is easy. Just find the ratio between the assessment and the price you paid for it. If you didn't buy it recently, it will be a little harder. First find a house that has been sold recently and is as much like your own as possible. (Assessors call this a "comparable.") The sales price should be roughly what your own home would sell for. Better still, find a number of "comparables" and find the average of their sales price. The ratio of your assessment to the sales price of these comparables you can consider your own assessment-sales ratio. A check on this method is to ask real estate brokers to estimate what price your house would bring, if it were placed on the market.

Next you need to find the assessment-sales ratio for other

homes in your community. First, find out which ones have been bought recently. If you know of a good number already, that will save some work. Otherwise, ask a realtor for lists he received, sometimes called a "multiple listing service," or for back copies of the special newspapers which in some areas are printed for real estate dealers. Information on property sales may also be available in bound volumes in the public library, or on the real estate page of your local newspaper. Or why not just ask the assessor himself?

If all these sources fail, you may yourself have to go through the deeds for property in your community to find the ones that have changed owners. By pinpointing those advertised over a two- or three-month period, however, this job can be made much easier.

These sources should show the sales prices of the properties. Find the ratio of assessment to sales price for each one, and then find the average. Compare this average ratio to the one for your own home. If yours is very much higher —say, 10 percent or more—the assessor should hear from you soon.

YOUR NEIGHBORHOOD COMPARED TO OTHER NEIGHBORHOODS

But what if *everyone* in your neighborhood is overassessed, compared to people in another neighborhood? Then, even if you checked your assessment against your neighbors', everything would seem O.K. The injustice wouldn't appear unless you compared the assessments in your neighborhood as a whole with those in other neighborhoods.

Most people aren't aware how common it is for assessors to hit one neighborhood harder than another. It happens all the time. And most often, it's the lower- and lower-middle-income taxpayers, and especially renters, that come out behind. Blacks get it worst. Studies in Boston, Philadelphia, Hartford, and other cities have shown that poor black neighborhoods are assessed much harder than well-to-do white ones. In Boston, the blacks were getting assessed over twice as hard!

Why does this happen? There are at least two reasons. First, assessors take the path of least resistance. Renters in general hardly ever get angry at the assessor—they don't see their assessment notice or tax bill. The landlord, who does get these, can pass any increases right along in the rent. Some leases even make the rent go up automatically when taxes go up. So landlords don't kick much either. But homeowners, who get their assessment notices and tax bills, and have to pay them, scream plenty. And the wealthier the homeowners, the more "connections" and "clout" they have and the more able they are to hire a lawyer. So some assessors try not to ruffle them. They go after the little guys instead.

The second reason is something called "assessment lag." Assessment lag is when assessments aren't up to date; when they "lag" behind current market values. Except where assessors are really doing their job, assessments are usually at least a few years behind; in some parts of the country, they are twenty years behind or more!

Who benefits? Most often the well-off, and people who speculate in land. Property values change. In older and poorer neighborhoods, they may rise very slowly, or they may even fall. But in the wealthiest neighborhoods, and in "fringe" areas just starting to be developed, values shoot way up. So when assessments don't keep up with these changes, poorer neighborhoods end up bearing the richer neighborhoods' load.

This illegal favoritism is not hard to expose. All it takes is a simple "ratio study." And don't let that fancy term scare you. A "ratio study" just compares the assessment-sales ratios in different neighborhoods. It requires only a little fact-getting, and some fifth-grade arithmetic.

1. Decide which neighborhoods you want to compare. Mark these neighborhoods out on a map. If you can get

copies of the maps the assessor uses, these are best. They show the "tax parcel number" of each property. These maps will make it much easier to find which neighborhood a particular property is in, if the assessments rolls aren't arranged by street address.

2. Make a list of all the homes sold in each of these neighborhoods over a one- or two-year period and the sales prices. You can find out what properties have been bought and sold recently from the sources listed above: "multiple listing service," public library, newspapers, the assessor, information on deeds or on other public documents. If there were too many sales to work with, then pick a sample—say, every second or third one. Cull out any transfers which don't look like regular "arms-length" sales: such as a sale to a son or daughter because these may not show the real value of the property. And if you can, try to include homes that are as much alike as possible—all single-family, for example.

3. Next, find the property tax assessment for each of these properties.

4. Then find the average ratio of assessment to sales price for each neighborhood.

5. Finally, compare the average ratio for each neighborhood. Which ones are getting the biggest "break"? And which ones are getting socked the hardest?

You can compare assessment ratios by value of property, as well as by neighborhood. Just take all the sales you used above and group them according to sales price: you might make one category for homes that sold for between $10,000 and $15,000, another for homes that sold for between $15,000 and $20,000, and so on. Then find the average assessment-sales ratio and the homes in each category. Is the assessor hitting the low-value homes harder than the homes of wealthy people? This is common. It is called "regressive assessment," hitting small taxpayers harder than the wealthy. It is one of the reasons that reform of the assessing process would help make the property tax more fair.

Remember, the law says that the assessment ratio for *every* home and for *every* neighborhood should be the same.

If your whole neighborhood is assessed higher than another, or if you and people who own or rent property worth about as much as yours, are getting assessed higher than owners or renters of more valuable property, you may want to join together and file a single lawsuit, called a "class action." That way you can share the legal costs, instead of having to pay them all yourself.

YOUR PROPERTY COMPARED WITH
OTHER KINDS OF PROPERTY

There are several different *kinds* of property. Real property, or real estate, is one kind. "Personal" property, like household goods and business equipment, is another. "Intangible" property, like stocks and bonds, is a third. We are speaking here of "real" property. (More and more, intangible and personal property is getting off the hook completely, through exemptions. That just dumps still more of the tax load onto the homeowner.)

"Real" property in turn, falls into different classes. One way to "classify" real property would be: one—vacant land; two—farms; three—single-family residences; four—two-family homes and small apartment buildings; five—large apartment buildings; six—small commercial buildings; seven—large commercial buildings; eight—small industrial properties; nine—large industrial properties.

In most states, the law says that *every* class of property should be assessed the same as all the others. But the assessor may be letting a class of property off light, while really socking it to homeowners of some other class. High-rise apartments and vacant land often get this broad-scale break. Commercial and industrial properties get the breaks too, but often on a one-by-one basis rather than as a whole class.

Laying bare this kind of assessment break is much like exposing it for a whole neighborhood. It too takes an assessment-sales ratio study. But instead of comparing the ratios in one neighborhood with those in another, you compare the average ratios for the different classes of property.

All of which sounds much more complicated than it really is.

Start with a list of the types of property in your community, or perhaps just the types you want to compare. Then, check the sources listed above for the properties in each class that were bought and sold recently. Take a random sample if there were too many to work with, and leave out any transfers that look unusual—not "arms-length." Next figure out the average assessment-sales ratio for each *class* of property. Is any class of property getting off easy, or getting hit extra hard?

Note that it may be hard to find recent sales for certain kinds of property, such as large commercial and industrial, since these are not bought and sold very often. Even if you can find one or two sales, this would not be enough to make a valid "sample." In that case, don't try to figure out an average ratio for the whole class. Instead, look for under-assessments of individual properties through sales data or in the ways-outlined above.

Note, too, that in a few states, the law sets different assessment ratios for different classes of property. Tennessee, for example, recently amended its constitution so that now public utility property is assessed at 55 percent of full market value, commercial and industrial property 40 percent, and residential and farm property 25 percent. Minnesota is another state with a "classified" property tax. In such a case, do not compare the average assessment ratios for each class of property with the others, but with what the law says the ratio for each class should be.

These are just three basic ways to find out whether the assessor is treating you and your neighbors fairly. As you begin to get a "feel" for property tax assessments, you will be able to use it in other ways as well. How much, for example, have the assessments on different kinds of property increased over the last five or ten years? Has the assessor been increasing them on one or more types but not on others? Do commercial and industrial property make up as large a share of the tax base (the total of all the assessments) as they did ten years ago? If not, why not? These are some of the questions you will be able to answer. They will help you to see who is calling the tune in your community—and how.

Tax Action

So, you have uncovered assessment inequities, a real scandal. It's all there in black and white in your report. Great? Well, maybe. No matter how *glaring* the abuses are, just your knowing about them won't change anything. If you want change, you have to put this information to work to get it.

How? Here are some of the ways taxpayers like yourself across the country have put property tax studies to work to get reform.

1. Issue the report through a press conference and press release. Distribute as many copies as possible. (You might even be able to charge enough for it to cover your expenses.)

2. Send a letter with your report and findings to the state attorney general, or to some other official who can and should do something about them. Be sure to send copies of the letter to other officials as well. Issue a press release, and call a press conference if possible.

3. Join with your neighbors in a "class action" lawsuit. Or go *together* to the assesor's office to demand that he explain the inequity, or to file appeals.

4. "Picket" or "demonstrate" outside the office of the assessor or other local official; or outside the offices or plant of a business that is getting a big tax break.

("Picket" and "demonstration" have become dirty words to many people. They bring up mental pictures of "radicals" and "hippies". They shouldn't. These acts are among the oldest and finest traditions of American citizenship. Concerned citizens were "demonstrating" here long before U.S. Steel was a glimmer in Judge Gary's eye and long before General Motors even thought of making cars into sex objects. Expressing views in public is a citizen's basic right—and duty.

When a steel company spends thousands on full-page ads in national newspapers and magazines—as the Bethlehem Steel Corporation did recently—to proclaim itself to the public as a stalwart taxpayer, *that* is a demonstration. Don't let anyone—including yourself—tag you with the label "radical" or "rabblerouser" just because you can't afford such blue-chip ways of expressing your views, and have to use means the corporate limousine set finds uncouth.)

5. Announce a drive to vote out of office the assessor (if he is elected) and any other officials who have worked against fair taxes. And don't forget to make known your support *for* officials and candidates who have taken up the cause of tax fairness.

6. Try to get a state representative, or member of Congress, to hold hearings on the tax abuses. Use your findings to make a case for reform in the way the property tax laws are written and applied. And offer to work with reform-minded local officials and state representatives. Often they *want* to help but don't have the time or staff.

Actions like these have *worked;* they have gotten results. Or rather, people like yourself have used them to get results. You can too.

Get advice from as many people and groups as you can who have used property tax studies to get action. Their experience can help you. The Tax Reform Research Group can help, too. They have names of such people and groups, and information you can use. Their publication, *People and Taxes*, has news and ideas on tax reform, and tells what people like yourself are doing about it. A sample copy is available from the Tax Reform Research Group, 733 15th Street N.W., Washington, D.C.

V

MAKING
GOVERNMENT
RESPONSIVE

A government that is shielded from its citizens tends to stagnate, to grow lazy and insensitive. Classic examples of do-nothing, unresponsive governments can often be found in "safe districts" where a party or a clique within a party has achieved absolute dominance over the electoral process. Equally flagrant examples can be observed in many government regulatory agencies. The personnel in these agencies are not elected; the public never has a chance to pass judgment on their performance. Regardless of which individual or party controls the government, the bureaucracy continues to function invisibly, silently, and inefficiently. Civil service regulations protect the incompetent, who in turn drive out the ambitious, the zealous, and those who "cause trouble" by doing their jobs too well.

Nader Study Group Reports on the Federal Trade Commission, the Interstate Commerce Commission, the Department of Agriculture, and other federal agencies and departments have demonstrated that lack of visibility and, more important, lack of accountability, have permitted federal agencies to ignore citizen needs, flout the law, and systematically sabotage the best-intentioned government programs. Incompetence and red tape do not account for all malfunctions in government agencies. Though ordinary citizens are unaware of the habits of bureaucrats, industries whose existence and profits are dependent on favorable government action are experts on bureaucratic operations. Because they are the only ones on the scene with the knowledge and resources to play a role in the shaping of policy, all too frequently government programs are tailor-made to industry demands—and often at citizen expense.

Civil service regulations also cause the government to be unresponsive. These regulations are ignored or strictly enforced, twisted or interpreted literally, at the pleasure of agency officials. In the hands of entrenched bureaucrats, transfers, promotions, department reductions, and other ordinary procedures, become tools for enforcing conformity to agency policy, often at the expense of efficiency or responsiveness to citizens. The civil servant quickly learns that the employee who blends in best, survives the longest. Those who dare to be different are transferred, isolated, downgraded, promoted to dead-end jobs, or expelled from government altogether.

Ultimately, of course, the citizen pays for these policies. Payment is sometimes made directly in the forms of higher taxes or reduced services. It is also made indirectly in the form of concessions to special-interest groups. Antitrust laxity costs consumers $25 billion a year in higher prices; income tax loopholes cost another $77 billion a year, property tax exemptions reduce local revenues by $6 billion per year; air pollution costs the nation $30 billion a year. More harmful are payments made in the currency of delays in imposing safety standards, understaffed legal aid or health programs, inadequate inspections of food and drugs, or delays in promulgating environmental controls. All of these are examples of government surrenders to private interests at citizen expense.

There is no clear remedy for these abuses. Where laws or

regulations have been violated, there is a possibility of court action. If legislative will has been thwarted, elected representatives can sometimes be prodded into taking action. But in the majority of cases the issue is not clear enough to arouse somnolent legislators and few people can afford to turn to the courts. More effective ways must be found to carry the citizen message to government.

The projects in this section are a start in that direction. Four deal with legislative functions, two with administrative functions, and one with the courts. Each individual project is useful. But ultimately, what is needed is a new relationship between citizen and government which will make government more responsive to citizen concerns.

How to Prepare
a Legislator's Scorecard

In the course of a two- or four-year term, a legislator may have to vote dozens of times on such issues as consumer protection, environmental preservation, equal opportunity, or tax reform. Although other legitimate factors may affect the outcome of an individual vote, the aggregate total of "yes" and "no" votes indicates the true measure of a legislator's concern for these particular issues. Rating the entire legislature on selected votes will produce a voting profile of how many elected officials support public-interest concerns. It will enable citizens to distinguish between rhetoric and reality and to measure their own representatives against other legislators. Used creatively, a rating of this sort can achieve considerable impact. No legislator today can be labeled "anticonsumer" or opposed to "environmental preservation" without losing votes.

A legislator's scorecard is easy to prepare. It is best to

concentrate on a single issue, like consumerism, though it is possible to combine two issues in the same rating to obtain "A Consumer and Environmental Voting Profile of Your State Legislators." To produce the survey, five to ten separate votes should be selected in which the lines between support and opposition are clearly drawn. For example, a vote against a state consumer agency or a truth-in-lending law, or in favor of letting a large corporation waive a safety standard would indicate anticonsumer bias.

It is important to remember that the most important vote is not necessarily a yea or nay on the question itself, but on what may seem to be a peripheral, procedural issue, such as a motion to table a recommendation to a legislative committee. These votes are not significant to the average layman, but often they are decisive and legislators base subsequent strategy and votes on them. Citizens preparing a scorecard should seek the help of someone familiar with the legislature—such as an experienced journalist or a lobbyist for consumer or environmental issues—to ensure that these crucial votes are not overlooked.

The second step is to go through the *Congressional Record*, city council minutes, or the state legislative record to place legislators in one of three categories on each vote—for, against, or not voting. The last category is important. Abstention can be a convenient means of ducking a critical vote. Frequent abstentions may indicate sloth or too great an involvement with other nonlegislative business.

After the survey is prepared, it should be circulated as widely as possible, calling special attention to legislators who are outstanding either for their support or opposition to the particular issues being studied. Normally the media will give good coverage to a legislative profile. If it is published in the midst of an election campaign, press coverage will be intensified.

The power of voting scorecards to effect change was demonstrated in 1970 when Environmental Action, the organizers of Earth Day, labeled as the "Dirty Dozen" twelve congressmen who had consistently voted against environmental preservation. When seven of the twelve were subsequently defeated in the general election, Congress gained new respect for environmental activists, and citizens obtained proof that the profile tactic was effective. In 1972 the campaign to defeat a new selection of environmentally insensitive congressmen was not as effective. Between the primaries and the general election only four of the Dirty Dozen were unseated. However, one of those defeated was Gordon Allott, chairman of the Senate Interior Committee.

The Dirty Dozen campaign succeeded because its organizers were careful to choose districts where the incumbent could be defeated and where awareness of environmental issues was high. They did not select impregnable one-party districts or districts where environmental concerns were not important. They rated legislators on issues which the average voter could understand. Most importantly, they used local environmental groups to distribute their ratings to newspapers, radio, and television stations, and to civic organizations within their chosen districts. They were further aided by the publicity the national media gave to their campaign.

An example of a voting profile of congressmen on environmental issues can be obtained from the League of Conservation Voters, 612 C Street, S.E., Washington, D.C. 20003; or from The Americans for Democratic Action, 1424 16th Street, N.W., Washington, D.C. 20036. The Americans for Constitutional Action, 955 L'Enfant Plaza North, S. W., Suite 1000, Washington, D.C. 20024, also puts out legislative analyses of voting records. Wisconsin's Environmental Decade, Box 117, Racine, Wisconsin, in cooperation with the Sierra Club and other environmental groups, prepared an excellent chart detailing the environmental voting records of all members of the Wisconsin State Senate and Assembly. They will send a free copy upon receipt of a request accompanied by a stamped, self-addressed envelope.

The release of the first voting profile should not signal an end to this project. Instead, it should mark the beginning of an effort to open government to greater citizen

scrutiny and participation. There should be follow-up efforts
to inform citizens of their legislators' votes on important
issues and to alert them to upcoming issues. When the legislature is in session, an interested citizen group can distribute weekly scorecards to interested civic organizations
and the media. Eventually, voting scorecards and previews
of future votes can join stockmarket quotations and base-
ball team standings as regular features in newspapers and
media news shows. The group compiling this information
should receive an added benefit of favorable coverage and
recognition in the community.

How to Form a Citizens' Lobby

"Lobbying," according to *Webster's New World Dictionary*,
"is an attempt to get legislatures to vote for a measure."
In a sense, any time a citizen writes a congressman or legislator or visits his office to urge him to support or oppose
a bill, that person is lobbying. Legally, however, a person
becomes a "lobbyist" only when he or she is paid a fee for
lobbying. In this technical sense, there are very few professional lobbyists representing consumer, environmental,
tax reform, or other broad citizen concerns. It is not difficult to understand why this is so. Professional lobbying is
expensive and most citizen groups cannot afford to pay the
salary and expenses of a full-time lobbyist.

The same is not true of numerous other groups. These
"special interests" are the major business corporations, large
labor unions, trade associations, and professional societies.
Because they may have a significant economic stake in the
outcome of particular votes, they are willing to station full-
time lobbyists, often with lavish expense accounts, in Washington and at various state legislatures. These men and
women are on the scene full-time, talking, dining, or golf-

ing with elected officials, arranging trips on company planes, getting tickets to the theater or to sports events for legislators or their aides, helping overworked staffs draft bills, providing studies and statistics, and making themselves generally useful. *The Washington Lobby*, a report compiled by *Congressional Quarterly*, gives a comprehensive review of legislation dealing with lobbying as well as case studies of major lobbying efforts.*

Their full-time presence gives these lobbyists enormous advantages. Because they are known, they are assured greater access to legislators than ordinary constituents without special credentials. And of course, they know what legislation is developing. Often, by the time a piece of legislation begins to be discussed publicly, it has already been shaped to fit the needs of the special-interest group it affects. This is also true of administrative rules and regulations. The average citizen acting individually has little chance of affecting this process. He is lucky if he even knows it is going on. On the other hand, the professional lobbyist is paid to know when new programs are being readied and how to shape their development.

Along with their full-time presence, special-interest lobbyists have other significant advantages. The average citizen can offer a legislator a single vote, possibly a small campaign contribution, and perhaps some kind words to neighbors and friends. But big business and big labor can offer much more in exchange for a legislator's vote. Aside from numerous small favors, they can promise sizable campaign contributions in the form of manpower and money. For a legislator facing a strong election challenge, these can be powerful lures, difficult to resist.

Occasionally, as in the defeat of the SuperSonic Transport (SST), an outpouring of citizen support shows what citizen lobbying can accomplish. But an SST fight can be

---

* *The Washington Lobby* can be obtained for four dollars by writing to *Congressional Quarterly*, 1735 K Street, N.W., Washington, D.C. 20006.

waged only once or twice a year. Legislators themselves can be rallied only a couple of times a session to "go to the mat" in an all-out confrontation. It is even more difficult to mobilize repeated citizen crusades. The result is that even if special-interest lobbyists lose a battle now and then, they have the staying power to outlast most citizen efforts.

An individual letter writer can sometimes influence a congressman, if the letter is especially persuasive or for some other reason catches the congressman's attention. But a single letter is no match against a live lobbyist armed with promises of campaign resources. Thousands of letters from concerned citizens to congressmen and newspapers can sometimes overcome numerous live lobbyists, as the SST fight proved; legislators have a keen sense of survival. Newspaper stories can have an even more powerful effect. Except in one-industry company towns, the smaller the body of government, the greater the influence of individual citizens. At the town level, there usually are no full-time lobbyists, and even though some citizens may get a more respectful hearing than others, anyone who cares to can be heard. The same is true in most small cities. In larger cities or at the county, state, or federal levels, you will have to work to be heard.

The first task is to organize. Basically, the same procedures that are used to form a citizen action club (see pp. 213–216) can be employed to launch a lobby. The organizers can be neighbors, friends, or co-workers; though they should be in agreement on the issue that brings them together, they certainly need not be members of the same political party. If you already have an organization—a consumer or environmental group, a women's club, or whatever—you can easily make it over into a lobbying group, provided the organization is not set up as a tax-deductible institution. (Tax-deductible institutions are not permitted to engage in a substantial amount of lobbying if they wish to retain their favored tax status.) The group need not be large—ten or twenty people can be surprisingly influential in local government, and a successful citizens lobby will grow naturally over time. Nor does the group need lavish newsletters or frequent meetings or expensively printed reports. It does need a "phone tree." This is not an exotic plant. It is a way to spread information swiftly: A calls B, C, D, and E; in turn, B calls F, G, H, and I; C calls J, K, L, and M; and so forth.

Although the group will have organized around some large issue—environment, women's rights, tax reform, etc.— it should quickly narrow its focus, lobbying on only one or two bills. The more concentrated the effort, the more effective the group is likely to be. Once the issues are decided upon, members of the group should be assigned to monitor the legislature in the particular area of interest, studying the relevant bills carefully to learn the pros and cons of each. Proposed federal legislation is reported on regularly in the *Washington Post*, but the best source of information on issues before Congress is the *Congressional Record*. The *Record* is published daily when Congress is in session. Many libraries subscribe to the *Record* and individual subscriptions are available for forty-five dollars a year from the Government Printing Office, North Capital Street, Washington, D.C. 20402.

State legislatures and city councils seldom publish proceedings, but elected representatives can be asked to inform the lobbying group of proposed legislation and upcoming bills. For local issues, members of the group can attend council meetings regularly to watch legislators in action and to monitor closely the progress of bills in which the group is interested.

Communication in the form of a simple one-sentence letter saying "Vote for ———" or "Vote against ———" carries little weight with legislators. Neither do form letters or statements clipped out of newspaper advertisements. But carefully thought-out letters *can* have an impact, especially on an issue that is not one the legislator is committed to support or oppose. It is in this middle area that lobbying is most useful. But to act effectively, members of the lobbying group must be well-informed, and must act before a position solidifies.

Occasionally, when an issue is important, the group may wish to take a more active role in the debate than mere letter writing or telegram sending. There are various ways to intensify the lobbying group's effect. A personal visit to the state capital to lobby is one way to increase impact; another is to request assistance from citizen groups working in allied areas. Support from large, well-established organizations such as unions, service clubs, or business associations is also helpful. So is editorial support from the press. The lobbying groups can conduct a public education effort by speaking before community organizations, writing articles for community newsletters, or sponsoring public meetings at which guest speakers can advocate the favored position. By undertaking a specific action project, the lobby can perform a useful service and at the same time attract support for its cause.

As the group grows stronger, it can form a working alliance with similar groups within the state. Eventually, if a coalition develops, it may be possible to unify and coordinate these part-time efforts by hiring a state coordinator on a temporary or full-time basis. But the place to start is not with a statewide effort (unless a well-funded citizen action group exists), but on the grass-roots level with small groups. When these groups achieve strength, they will expand. And the state lobby that eventually grows up will be all the stronger for its local ties. Information on state lobbies can be obtained from the Citizen Action Group, 2000 P Street N.W., Washington, D.C. 20036.

How to Convene and Hold Citizen Hearings

Periodically, legislative and administrative bodies hold hearings at which statements are presented by other government officials, private experts, interested parties, or average citizens. Hearings are held for various reasons. Sometimes they are part of a legislative investigation to determine whether a particular government agency, law, or regulation is effective. At other times, hearings are convened to determine whether new laws or new regulations are needed and what the effects of these might be. If the Federal Communications Commission, for example, wanted to impose obligations on broadcasters which would increase the air time allocated to news and public service programs, or if the commission were thinking about banning certain products such as cigarettes from advertising over the air, it would probably hold hearings to determine the effect these measures would have on the broadcasting industry.

Some hearings, especially those held by committees without the power to propose new legislation, are held purely to publicize certain facts or to determine the facts in a controversy. For example, Senator William Proxmire's Joint Economics Committee regularly holds hearings to call attention to government waste. On the other hand, hearings sometimes are called to defuse an explosive subject by drowning it in a sea of conflicting and confusing testimony. The 1972 ITT hearings are a good example of this tactic.

A citizens group can use appearances at government hearings, both legislative and administrative, to further the public interest. Carefully prepared testimony may influence the government body and convince it to follow a particular course of action. Since all testimony becomes part of the legislative record, it can have an important impact later on, if the hearing record is examined. Appearances at government hearings can also be used to dramatize the intensity and scope of citizen concern with an issue. When hundreds of Connecticut citizens answered the Connecticut Citizen Action Group's appeal and jammed meeting halls in which state hearings on proposed clean air standards were being held, commissioners received a powerful message in support of strong standards.

Frequently, agencies or legislative committees refuse to consider controversial issues which acutely affect public well-being. Hearings sometimes are stalled by a single committee chairman who has the power to block an investigation. Or, if hearings are held, they may ignore the citizen perspective and merely rubber-stamp an arrangement favorable to one or more powerful special interests. In such a situation, the only avenue left open to citizen activists is to protest the government's action or lack of action. Protest can come in the form of letters, phone calls, picketing or partisan electoral activity. But one of the best ways to focus public attention on the abuse at the time it occurs is to convene a citizens' panel to do what government was supposed to do.

Obviously, a citizen hearing can never replace government action. Citizens have no right to investigate other private individuals and a citizen body cannot subpoena individuals or information. Nor can it enact legislation or pass binding regulations. Moreover, it is important to use this tactic only when circumstances are appropriate. Too frequent use dulls its impact; incorrect use discredits both the hearings and the citizen group sponsoring them. But even with these limitations, there is much that a citizen hearing can accomplish, especially when it is probing into government activities.

For example, the Connecticut Citizen Action Group convened citizen hearings in New London, Connecticut, on March 24, 1972, three days after an oil spill fouled the waters and beaches around that city. Prior to the hearings, public attention had been focused on how citizens could clean up the mess. But testimony at the CCAG hearings offered by lobster fishermen, sportsmen, resort owners, environmentalists, professors, students, state legislators, and town officials switched the focus away from the futile task of trying to clean up #2 fuel oil, which sinks to the sea bottom, to a search for who was to blame and how to avoid a similar tragedy in the future. The hearings received wide publicity on radio and television and were covered on page one of the *New London Day*. The role of the Coast Guard, which refused to attend the CCAG hearings, came under question. The press began to ask why the Coast Guard had not enforced its own regulations. Even though a later Coast Guard court of inquiry blamed the tanker captain, many New London citizens paid more attention to the evidence uncovered by the citizen investigators. Partly as a result of these hearings, other actions by the Navy and the Coast Guard are coming under scrutiny. In Groton, citizens aided by CCAG accused the Navy of flouting the National Environmental Policy Act by polluting the water with raw sewage. The CCAG hearings, in short, provided a launching pad for a continuing citizen movement.

The Citizen Action Project (CAP) in Chicago offers a more dramatic illustration of what can result from citizen hearings. CAP's primary purpose is to use hearings as an organizing focus to rally citizen support. The hearings also serve as a sounding device to register citizen sentiment and in some cases to dramatize a particular issue. For example, on February 13, 1972, CAP sponsored a "taxpayers assembly" that brought together citizen groups and individuals who had attended one or more evenings of citizen hearings held prior to the assembly in different neighborhoods in Chicago. The assembly focused on property tax abuse, waste by the Board of Education, and plans to stop a proposed expressway. Some of the citizen action efforts launched at the assembly are still underway. Others have registered impressive successes. A property-tax rebate program for senior citizens designed in part by CAP and later endorsed by former Governor Richard Ogilvie passed the state legislature. CAP's role in the expressway fight was even more impressive. Because of public attention generated by the hearings and other demonstrations, the expressway became an issue in the gubernatorial race. A ward-by-ward organizing effort by concerned citizens along the entire twenty-two-mile proposed corridor captured 60,000 votes for Daniel Walker. On the day after his election to the governorship, he announced the cancellation of the expressway—a clear victory for CAP and the numerous citizen activists working with it.

Any citizens group which undertakes to hold public hearings should realize the extent of preparation needed to insure success. The subject of the hearings has to be researched thoroughly. This will determine who the witnesses should be, the level of their expertise, their biases, and their willingness to cooperate with a citizen group. In addition, a number of administrative details must be settled, such as the timing, location, specific focus, and procedures of the hearings, and the composition of the panel.

Timing. Ordinarily, hearings should be held at a time when interest in a subject is still building. Unless new evidence is available it serves no purpose to hold citizen hearings after a subject has been thoroughly examined by regular government hearings. However, a citizen panel can be used to initiate consideration of a matter.

Generally, hearings should last no longer than a few days to avoid wearing out the public's reception. Since public attention is one of the main purposes of the hearings, day-to-day scheduling should take into account newspaper and broadcast media deadlines.

Location. The hearings should be held in a place that is both easily accessible to the press and public and appropriate to the issue. For instance, if lead paint poisoning in ghetto housing is being studied, the hearings should not be conducted in a plush midtown hotel. Wherever the hearing is held, arrangements should be made to handle the press, witnesses, and any unexpected problems such as illness, accident, or overflow crowds. A citizen group can minimize expenses by holding the hearings at a church, a school, or other free facility.

Specific Purpose and Procedures. Hearings run haphazardly may be worse than no hearings at all, since they will do more to confuse than to inform, leaving a bad impression of the hearing sponsors and, by implication, of the cause they espouse. Sloppy hearings sap energy that could have been channeled elsewhere. To prevent a rambling discussion, a specific focus should be determined. Advance notice should be given to all witnesses of the amount of time alloted to each and of what is required of them. Wherever possible, witnesses should be required to submit a written statement in advance. A court reporter should be engaged to take down all the statements or the hearings should be tape recorded. If this is not practical, several volunteer secretaries should be engaged to prepare a record of the proceedings.

Hearing Panel. The make-up of the panel is critical to the success of the hearings. At least some of the panelists should have expertise in the area under consideration and, if possible, at least one panelist should be a lawyer. The chairman of the meeting should be experienced at handling unruly witnesses or possible audience interruptions and should strictly control all procedures. Questions from the chair and cross-examination can be used to draw out testimony.

After all the testimony is gathered, the panel should sum up, draw conclusions, and make recommendations for future action. If interest in the hearings has been high, the panel should present its conclusions and recommendations at a special press conference called for that purpose. The press conference is the climax of the hearings and should be the final action taken by the hearing panel.

The hearings themselves may accomplish the purpose of the citizens group if they force a government agency to take action. If they do not, the group must decide what further steps will lead to implementation of the panel's recommendations. If evidence of criminal conduct was uncovered, it should be turned over to the local prosecuting attorney or attorney general. The citizens group may appeal to the courts to right a civil wrong, or use the success of the hearings to marshal greater public support which may force legislative action at some future time. These are tactical decisions that will vary in each situation, but some positive steps should be taken to avoid much talk, a few headlines, but no real change.

How to Organize an Initiative

An *initiative* is a procedure enabling voters to propose a law and pass it by themselves. Fifteen states, at present, give the people the right to originate legislation by means of the initiative. Several also permit constitutional amendments to be proposed in the same way, though more citizen support is usually required for amendments.

The initiative is a powerful tool because it permits a group of citizens to go over the heads of legislators and appeal directly to the people for support. It is most useful when citizens are confronted by a lethargic, do-nothing legislature or one captured by special-interest groups. An initiative should not be attempted, however, unless it is certain that ordinary legislative channels have failed. Even then, an initiative campaign should not be undertaken lightly, since it is a difficult effort to organize successfully. Just getting on the ballot requires petitions from 6 percent,* 7 percent,† 8 percent,‡ or 10 percent§ of those who voted

---

* Oregon.
† Nebraska.
‡ Arkansas, California, Colorado, Florida, Illinois, Michigan, Mississippi, Oklahoma.
§ Arizona, Nevada, Ohio.

in the last election. Missouri, Nebraska, and Nevada further complicate the job of citizen activists by requiring that a certain percentage of the signatures collected must be in a specified number of counties or congressional districts. Massachusetts puts additional hurdles in the way. Nevertheless, if lobbying, persuasion, or electoral challenges fail to move a recalcitrant legislature, an initiative may be a citizen's last recourse. (Of course, thirty-five states do not permit initiatives. Citizen action groups should lobby for this important safeguard for citizen rights. In some states initiatives can be permitted by statute; others may require an amendment to the state constitution.)

Those experienced in waging initiative battles stress that one of two conditions is required for success. Either the proposition must be so popular that people flock to support it or the citizen group must have a strong organization capable of spreading word of the petition and capturing support. The less glamorous the initiative measure, the more necessary it is to have a strong organization.

Initiative drives in Colorado during 1972 illustrate both situations. The Colorado Project of Common Cause, using a superb state organization, managed to collect enough signatures to place four propositions on the ballot. The measures dealt with important issues such as no-fault automobile insurance, property tax reform, the public utility commission, and a state freedom of information law. At no time did these measures excite widespread public attention and three of them eventually were turned down at the polls. On the other hand, the initiative to ban the Olympics from Colorado was sponsored by an ad hoc coalition of concerned citizens whose only purpose was to stop the Olympics. Even though the organization itself was weak, the measure generated so much attention and support that it was able to gain a place on the ballot and to carry in the November election.

The anti-Olympic initiative is a case study of how to organize a campaign around a controversial issue. The drive had its beginnings in late 1971 and first received public attention in January, 1972, when organizers sent out 6,000 letters to citizens and environmental groups asking for their help and requesting them to sign a petition opposing the Colorado site for the Olympics. Many signed petitions and about 800 volunteers offered to help. These petitions were presented to the Olympic Committee in Japan (where the 1972 Winter Games were underway), but were summarily rejected.

On March 29, petitions to place an initiative on the ballot were mailed to all those who had responded to the January letter and to new recruits brought in by the March 15 press release. The campaign picked up momentum throughout the spring and early summer and on July 6, 77,392 signatures were submitted to the secretary of state. This figure exceeded the required signature total by 25,000 names—a sure indication that the measure had popular support. During the rest of the summer and through the election campaign, the initiative organizers did not slacken. The final vote opposing the Colorado site won by a margin of 60 to 40 percent of those voting.

Whether your issue is high-voltage or low-voltage, there are several steps you can take to increase its chances of turning on the voters. First, make yourself completely familiar with the state law governing initiative. In election law, technicalities are elevated to the status of sacred principles. Even the smallest error in the wording of the petition or the method of collection may invalidate months of effort. Special attention should be paid to the requirements governing who can circulate and who can sign petitions, whether or not signatures have to be in ink, and if they must duplicate exactly the name under which the voter is registered (i.e., John Smith might be invalid if Mr. Smith is registered under the name John G. Smith.) The citizen group can receive helpful information on election law from the secretary of state, but it is also a good idea to seek the advice of a lawyer familiar with petition procedures. More than one seemingly successful petition drive has been invalidated because of faulty collection procedures.

The second critical factor is that the law which the group is seeking to have adopted must be very carefully drafted. Nothing would be more discouraging to activists or more destructive of citizen confidence than to complete a successful petition drive, win the election campaign, and then have the entire effort vitiated by court action declaring the measure unconstitutional. Here law professors and constitutional lawyers can be of immense help. If another state has a similar statute whose constitutionality has been tested, it can provide a model for the new initiative measure.

Phrasing must be as simple and precise as possible to avoid confusing the average voter. A few years ago voters in New York City wishing to establish a civilian review board to oversee police activities had to vote no on the proposition because of its deceptive wording. In effect, a no vote constituted a yes vote in favor of the measure. Bad drafting can needlessly complicate the measure in other ways. A proposed 1972 California antipornography statute was so vaguely worded that it could be construed to ban not only X-rated movies, but most movies and many television shows presently in production. As a result, many who supported some type of legislation to control pornography were forced to oppose the measure and it failed.

Once the measure has been drafted and the technicalities of election law fulfilled, organizers must devise a campaign strategy. Usually the law specifies a time period during which signatures can be collected. Long before this period the group organizing the drive must determine how the measure will be presented to the public, what other groups will be asked to cosponsor it, and who will be recruited to aid the group in areas where it is weak.

Media coverage is a key element in the success of any initiative drive. Most people are reluctant to sign a petition for a proposition they have never heard of. This is especially true in states where the initiative is infrequently used.

Therefore media coverage must be aggressively sought. When the campaign is started, it should be announced at press conferences in the state capital and the state's largest cities. These should be followed by appearances on radio and television talk shows, speeches before community groups, letters to newspapers, distribution of flyers, pamphlets, and other attention-getting efforts.

The drive for press coverage should be intensified as the signatures themselves are being collected. Shopping centers, large apartment houses, churches, social and sports events should be thoroughly canvassed. A certain number of committed petitioners should be kept ready to shore up areas where the drive may weaken. The petition solicitation should be as thorough as possible and smoothly executed. The first few thousand signatures will probably be rather easily obtained. The last ones are almost always the most difficult.

The drive should not slacken once the requisite number of signatures has been obtained. On the contrary, several thousand additional signatures should be sought as insurance. If a special-interest group feels threatened by the initiative, it will almost certainly go to court and seek to have all or some of the petitions invalidated on technicalities. Therefore, it is important to build up a cushion so that if some signatures are invalidated, sufficient numbers will still be counted to get the measure on the ballot. The petitioning campaign should be regarded an an educational effort, informing the electorate of the initiative to be voted on in the coming election. The more signatures, the greater the chance of an election victory.

The final step in the initiative drive after the petition has won a place on the ballot is the campaign for approval by the electorate. The fight for approval must take on all of the trappings of a good political campaign, except that instead of a flesh and blood candidate, an issue is seeking to win majority support. All candidates standing for office should be asked to take a position on the measure, though the initiative must remain as separate as possible from the personalities of individual candidates to avoid its becoming a partisan issue. Editorial support should be sought from newspapers, radio, and television stations. Finally, a drive to bring voters to the polls should be organized.

Freedom of Information: The First Essential

Everyone remembers the familiar scene repeated over and over in one form or another on issues ranging from the war to pollution to tax reform. A television commentator conducting interviews on a busy street asks a citizen what he or she thinks of a particular government policy. The person replies, "I have to back the government. I don't have the facts and they do."

Before citizens can begin to watchdog government, they must be able to gain access to government information. Sometimes information is needed as an end in itself. Oftentimes it is needed to provide background and support for substantive legal or publicity activities. Whatever the reason, citizens have a right to know how the government is discharging its responsibilities.

The Freedom of Information Act (5 USC § 552) guarantees the public's right of access to federal government information. (Many states have similar laws.) Under the act a citizen has a right to see any document, file, or other record held by a federal government agency, except documents protected by nine exemptions to the act, two of them extremely minor. However, the government, not the person seeking access, has the burden of proving that a document fits one of the following exemptions.

—Specifically required by executive order to be kept

secret in the interest of the national defense or foreign policy;

—Related solely to the internal personnel rules and practices of an agency;

—Specifically exempted from disclosure by statute;

—Trade secrets and commercial or financial information obtained from a person and privileged and confidential information;

—Interagency or intraagency memoranda or letters which would not be available by law to a party other than an agency in litigation with an agency;

—Personnel and medical files and similar files, the disclosure of which would constitute a clearly unwarranted invasion of personal privacy;

—Investigatory files compiled for law enforcement purposes except to the extent available by law to a party other than an agency;

Disputes over access to information revolve around interpretations of these exemptions, especially the second, fourth, and fifth. But citizens should remember that it is up to the government to assert and prove that a document is exempted.

A request for information must be in writing and identify as clearly as possible the documents requested. The reasons why the document is needed do *not* have to be specified. The request should ask for an answer within thirty days and, if none is received, the request should be considered to have been denied. A telephone call or two to the agency sometimes will speed up procedures. If a request is denied an appeal should be made to the head of the agency. An appeal letter should repeat the request (attach a copy of the original letter) and state that an appeal is being made. The appeal letter itself only has to be two or three sentences long. If the appeal is denied the only recourse is to turn to the United States District Court which has the power to review the denial.

To help citizens obtain information, Ralph Nader's Center for Study of Responsive Law has established the

Freedom of Information Clearinghouse. The Clearinghouse will provide advice and legal assistance to citizens struggling to obtain access to government information. Examples of the type of information that citizen groups might wish to obtain are the following:

—State and federal meat inspection reports;
—Internal Revenue Service agent manuals;
—Occupational Safety and Health inspection manuals;
—Federal inspection reports of many types;
—Nursing home survey reports;
—Government test results on product testing;
—Civil rights compliance reports.

Requests for assistance should be addressed to the Freedom of Information Clearinghouse, P. O. Box 19367, Washington, D.C. 20036.

How to Evaluate Government Inspection Systems

Federal, state, and local government agencies regularly conduct inspections of safety and health conditions affecting the public welfare. They also monitor such environmental conditions as air quality, water purity, and noise levels. The shopper feels secure when meat is stamped "U.S.D.A. approved." People take medication confident that the prescription has been adequately tested and the manufacturing process rigidly controlled. Workers depend on government inspection to protect their safety and health at work. The cars people drive, the homes and apartments they live in, the plants they work in, the planes they fly in, the food they eat, the water they drink, and dozens of other items are subject to government regulation and inspection. Some must be inspected, by law or by agency regulation. Others may be inspected at the discretion of agency officials. In a few cases, inspections occur only when they are specifically requested by an affected party.

Citizens rely heavily on government inspections to protect their health and safety. And, as society and technology grow more complex, the citizen will have to rely more than ever on government inspection and quality certification to protect his health and welfare.

From all available evidence, government inspection has been a flop in all too many instances. Nader Study Group Reports over the past four years have detailed instance after instance of government negligence or abdication to private corporations in this area, and reports from other sources have provided further information. After passage of the Mine Safety Act the Bureau of Mines still conducted only 31 percent of the safety and only 1 percent of the health inspections required by the law in two of the most important mining districts in the United States. The National Highway Traffic Safety Administration delayed its investigations three years before demanding the recall of millions of 1968–69 Chevrolets with engine mount defects; Department of Agriculture meat and poultry inspections have been repeatedly cited as inadequate by private investigators as well as by the General Accounting Office. When the failures of state and local inspections are added to those of the federal government, the problem becomes even more serious.

The inspection problem is really two problems: making sure thorough inspections take place, and making sure the evidence they discover is made public and is acted upon. Examples of suppression and failure to act abound. The Pesticide Regulation Division of the Department of Agriculture did nothing for sixteen years after it became aware of safety problems with lindane vaporizers; the Federal Communications Commission refused to release an important staff memorandum to the public even as passages from it were being quoted in industry trade magazines.

The Justice Department has consistently refused to prosecute known antitrust violators. The General Accounting Office found that the Bureau of Mines had, on its own initiative, reduced fines for safety and health violations to one twenty-fifth of the amount formerly required; the fines became only twenty dollars for violations resulting in imminent danger to life and a mere four dollars for violations caused by an unwarranted failure to comply with the Mine Safety Act. These amounts are scandalously small. In fact, it pays a company *not* to take precautions if fines are too low or penalties sporadically enforced. *The Spoiled System*, a recent Nader Report on the Civil Service Commission written by Robert Vaughn, concludes that such government laxity is "the most massive and systematic violation of laws in the United States."

Surely industry is not about to call for more enforcement of government regulations—so it is up to citizens to take the initiative to protect their own welfare. The first step is to collect data on present government inspection programs to determine whether they are carrying out their basic function. Certain questions are fundamental to this evaluation and they should be put to the head of the inspection division in the agency under investigation. An investigation of occupational health and safety inspection, for example, might start with these questions:

Question 1. How many establishments or locations is the division supposed to inspect?

Question 2. How many inspectors are there in all? How many of these are in the field.

Question 3. How frequently are inspections required? If there is no formal requirement, how often are they made?

The answers to these three questions provide the basis for a preliminary analysis. By dividing the answer to question 1 by the number of *field* inspectors in answer 2, a reasonable estimate can be made as to the likelihood of fulfilling the standard established in the answer to question 3.

The experience of a committee investigating safety and

health inspections in New York state illustrates the use of this technique.* The New York State Labor Department was charged with the duty of inspecting 226,800 workplaces in the state of New York. To carry out this job, its inspection service had 530 employees statewide but only 118 full-time field inspectors. The arithmetic indicated that if each establishment were to be visited once a year (the standard set by the department), each inspector would have to visit 1,900 sites a year, or 5 a day, seven days a week, fifty-two weeks a year. When weekends, holidays, vacations, sick leave, and routine paperwork were figured in, the task became even more implausible. Without probing more deeply it was possible to conclude at the very least that the department's own standard wasn't being met. At worst, it indicated the possible existence of uninspected hazards endangering the lives of thousands of working people in New York State.

One might go further and determine how many years it would take to inspect every workplace in the state at the current rate of inspection. After eight months of enforcement of the federal Occupational and Safety Health Act, for example, it was estimated that it would take 284 years to reach each of the nation's four million workplaces *just once* if the rate of inspection did not change or the number of inspectors was not increased. Even if calculations reveal that the targeted inspection schedule is feasible, there are other questions to raise.

If there is a required standard for the frequency of inspections (once a year or once every two years) then an obvious follow-up to the first three questions is:

Question 4. Are the required number of inspections actually made? It may well be that even with a staff of inspectors large enough to do the job, sloth, indifference, or bureaucratic red tape prevent the requisite number of inspections from being carried out.

* "Official Lawlessness in New York State: Disease and Death in the Industrial Environment," by Adam Walinsky, Robert Hemley, John McIlwain, Donald Ross.

A separate line of questioning can reveal the competence of the inspectors.

Question 5. What qualifications are needed by inspectors?

Question 6. What sort of training program is offered to new inspectors? How long is it and what does it entail?

Question 7. Is there a requirement for in-service training?

If qualifications are minimal and little training is provided, it is likely that the inspectors are not particularly competent and that the inspection function rates a low priority overall.

The next series of questions probes the worth of the inspections themselves.

Question 8. Do inspections follow a public schedule or do they take place unannounced (i.e., do establishments know when they are going to be inspected)?

Question 9. About how long does each inspection take?

Question 10. Who guides the inspector through the establishment—a worker, a supervisor, or both?

Question 11. Do inspectors have access to sophisticated monitoring equipment to detect health hazards?

Question 12. If so, do they regularly use it?

The purpose of question 8 should be obvious. Announced inspections allow the establishment to prepare for a visit, to cover up hazards, or to slow down production in order to decrease plant pollution. Questions 9 and 10 go to the same problem. If not more than a few minutes are spent in each establishment, only the most obvious faults can be detected. The same is true if a plant manager guides the inspector past potential hazards with no worker present to point out what is happening.

In Connecticut, when questions 11 and 12 were put to the head of the Occupational Health Department, the answer to 11 was "yes" while the answer to 12 was "no, good inspectors don't need it." When the doctor was then asked how "good inspectors" were able to detect carbon monoxide, which is colorless, odorless, tasteless, and otherwise undetectable to the unaided senses, he stated that good inspectors develop a "sixth sense" that enables them to spot it. Pity the workers protected by a sixth sense.

It is possible for the inspection process to fail even if a well-qualified inspector does a thorough job. This situation can occur when there are no procedures for correcting faults uncovered by inspectors, or when existing procedures are not enforced. The following questions can illuminate this situation.

Question 13. What procedure is followed if a violation is found during an inspection?

Question 14. What penalty (fine, suspension, license revocation, criminal prosecution) is imposed for a violation that is judged serious?

Question 15. Is there a follow-up inspection after a violation is discovered to see whether the hazard was corrected? How soon?

Question 16. Is there any special penalty for repeated violations or for a refusal to correct a violation?

Once these questions are answered, it is worthwhile to determine how much an average proposed penalty is. Calculating this figure may help to counteract industry statements that fines for noncompliance with health and safety regulations will put companies out of business. It will also show whether the penalty is stiff enough to serve as a deterrent.

Question 17. What was the total number of violations for noncompliance with safety and health laws in the previous years?

Question 18. What was the total amount of proposed penalties for violations?

Divide the answer in question 18 by that in question 17 to get the average dollar fine per violation. For example, under the federal Occupational Safety and Health Act, an employer can be fined up to $1,000 for a serious violation, though this rarely happens. In 1971, however, 35,839 violations were alleged with only $737,486 in fines proposed by the enforcement agency. The average penalty was about $23, a trivial sum even though many of the offenses were only technical violations. Such small fines might encourage companies to risk being found in noncompliance rather than spend money to make their plants safer.

The closing questions should determine the openness of the agency to more intense citizen monitoring.

Question 19. Are copies of written complaints filed by consumers or workers available to citizens?

Question 20. Can citizens obtain access to inspection reports? If the answer to either of these questions is no, the state "right to know" or "freedom of information law" should be examined to see if the refusal is illegal. Even if it isn't, citizen investigators should continue to try to gain access to this information. Newspapers can be valuable allies in fights to gain access to government documents.

There are other questions that can be added to this list to probe more deeply into the inspection. And, of course, the questions would be somewhat different for investigations of other inspection programs. Comparative studies can be undertaken to measure the strength of an inspection program against the strength of model inspection programs in other cities or states. But in general, without going into technical details involving scientific judgments about the worth of X testing method compared to Y method or the accuracy of one testing instrument over another, the questions above should enable the citizen activist to examine the worth of a city, state, or federal inspection program. We suggest, however, that to be truly effective, background information on the general area and the particular agency under study should be digested before beginning an evaluation.

When the evaluation is completed, it should be given to the agency and released to the public with findings and recommendations. Recommendations may ask for legislative hearings to determine why the agency is not fulfilling its inspection mission. More funds and personnel or an agency reorganization may be called for. In some cases, there may be grounds for a lawsuit.

More direct action is also possible. An evaluation of occupational health and safety inspections may be handed out to workers at factory gates and followed up by a union demand for better inspections. Shoppers entering butcher shops and supermarkets may be given reports on the quality of state meat inspections. Housing inspection deficiencies can be used to rally tenants. In every case the emphasis must be on turning the data gathered through the evaluation into an effective action program calculated to remedy whatever problems were found.

How to Investigate a Government Agency

One tactic which has proved especially useful in rousing bureaucracies to action is a citizen-sponsored investigation of a government agency followed by publication of the findings. Some investigations in the past have altered government policies. The Federal Trade Commission (FTC), for example, was transformed from a doormat for industry into a reasonably vigorous consumer representative, mostly as a result of a chain of events touched off by the publication of the Nader Study Group's report. Personnel changes, a tougher attitude toward fraudulent advertisers, and new attempts to involve consumers all can be traced to the study. But even where the results are not so dramatic, there are bound to be benefits from a citizen probe. The mere presence of informed citizen investigators within an agency, asking questions and reviewing documents, can have a positive effect on the behavior of bureaucrats.

Most citizens do not have the time or resources to embark on a major study of a federal agency. But they can probe a single department of a large agency. Investigators probing the Office of Defects Investigation, National Highway Traffice Safety Administration, have greatly changed that division's policies. At one time it conducted few defect investigations, kept its files closed to the public, and served mainly as a shield for the automobile industry. Today, although the division still lags in a number of important ways, it is conducting a number of defect investigations which are matters of public record, its files of complaint letters are open to public scrutiny, and as a result of its new posture, automobile recalls are on the increase. This division's turnabout is largely due to the stimulus of citizen investigators.

Local and state agencies are at least as susceptible to the stimulus of a citizen probe. Because of their smaller size and more limited jurisdictions and geographical proximity, they can be studied more easily. In Wallingford, Connecticut, a fifteen-page report on the activities of the tax assessor by the Connecticut Citizen Action Group touched off town hearings and an investigation by the mayor. As a result, the mayor formed new policies on citizen access to the assessor's records and those of other city offices. Several other studies by CCAG followed the same pattern: short, factual reports on specific agency activities followed by specific suggestions for reform.

Similar investigations by citizen teams from Public Interest Research Groups in other states have proved the effectiveness of this tactic. In Oregon, OSPIRG investigators probed the state Department of Agriculture's meat inspection program. The inadequacies they uncovered were instrumental in persuading the state to turn the inspection program over to the federal government. The Minnesota PIRG's toy safety study in early 1972 revealed gross inadequacies in the Food and Drug Administration's inspection system. To help remedy its weaknesses, the FDA embarked on an advertising campaign and helped citizen teams monitor toy safety in other states. Although FDA's response is still far from adequate, the fact that the agency moved at all attests to the impact of a twenty-five-page study of one state's experience which took only 2 weeks to complete.

The following pages outline procedures for a major investigation of an entire agency. Few groups will be capable of undertaking a study of this magnitude, but the same procedures, scaled down to fit the needs and resources of a citizen group, are valid whether the probe is of a town health department with two employees or a major state agency with several thousand employees.

The decision as to which agency should be investigated will usually be dictated by a combination of the investigator's interests and the obvious needs. But if a citizens group is uncertain, here is a suggestion that promises to yield useful results. A little-studied government function is that of the purchasing department for the city or state. Because it keeps a low public profile, government procurement is an area particularly susceptible to corruption and mismanagement. The school that purchases supplies in piecemeal fashion from a local stationery store is a typical example of mismanagement, since bulk purchases from wholesalers would undoubtedly save money. If the stationery store happens to be owned by a member of the school board, a strong presumption of a conflict of interest arises. Boss William Tweed managed to rob millions of dollars from New Yorkers by careful use of the city purchasing department in the 1860s and 70s. Other areas ripe for investigation are departments of occupational health and safety in an industrial region, bureaus of mines in mining areas, and insurance, banking, highway, and environmental and consumer agencies everywhere.

The team of investigators can be large or small, depending upon the agency or department in question. Training in law, government, economics, or business is helpful, but it is important to remember that average people with ordinary skills and no special training are quite capable of organizing and carrying out worthwhile studies. All that is required is persistence, accuracy, and common sense.

One person should be selected to serve as team leader and project director. If the study is a large one, codirectors or assistant directors may also be chosen. Discipline is critical. The team leader must oversee the whole project, assign individual tasks, and make sure they are completed. Sloppy procedures tend to produce a sloppy report.

Before the investigation itself begins, investigators should seek a pledge of cooperation from the head of the agency. Such a pledge guarantees access to agency information and personnel. It is also tactically wise; if the agency later decides not to cooperate because investigators are probing too deeply, it is forced on the defensive since it must go back on its word.

At the outset, it is important to gather background material dealing with the activities of the agency. Some can be obtained directly from the agency under investigation; others have to be dug out of newspaper files, library reference rooms, or the legislative record. The following checklist of materials should be useful: ·

—General background reading in the subject area plus general reference material;

—The enabling legislation which created the agency and all court decisions interpreting it;

—A copy of the agency's regulations;

—Copies of the agency's annual reports for the last five years;

—An annotated bibliography of law review articles dealing with different aspects of the agency's operations, if any (this can be compiled from the *Index of Legal Periodicals* found in all law libraries);

—An annotated bibliography of articles from trade magazines and one or two leading newspapers covering the agency (large public libraries should have most important trade journals);

—Transcripts of all congressional or state legislative hearings (usually available from the relevant legislative committees);

—Copies of governmental or private studies of the agencies, if any;

—All published speeches, press releases, or internal newsletters of the agency;

—All studies published by the agency;

—Studies by other government agencies which touch on the agency under investigation or aspects of its operations;

—Agency publications used for employment purposes, such as job descriptions or cost studies, which are used to justify budget requests;

—List of current personnel and their jobs.

This material should be read and digested before the public phase of the study begins. Team members should be assigned to particular areas of agency operations. They should circulate a steady stream of reports, comments, and observations to other members of the team so that information can be shared. It is the job of the team leader to read each of these reports and to develop an on-going strategy, including areas that should receive the greatest emphasis and lists of people to be interviewed.

Once the investigators are thoroughly familiar with agency operations, they should begin to conduct individual interviews with agency personnel. Since it is often impossible to obtain second interviews with agency personnel, all pertinent questions must be asked the first time around. When conducting interviews, a certain number of questions should be prepared before hand, but the investigator should be ready to pursue a different line of questioning if it appears suitable.

Investigators should not repeat a set format of questions in each interview. Questions should be mixed and the same question asked several times in different ways. It is often useful to add some assertions and then ask for comments: "I am told that X lobbyist was consulted before the agency promulgated its new rules. Is this true?" Another technique is to ask questions to which you already know the answer. For example, ask about the existence of a study which you have in your brief case. This way you can check whether the person is telling the truth. Also by discussing the contents, even though you supposedly don't have the study, you can appear to be even more informed than you are. In this way you may pick up additional facts which the person might normally conceal but which he thinks you know already.

Tape recording interviews may be permitted, though it is sometimes a mixed blessing. While it preserves precise information, it also may inhibit the interviewee so completely that no useful information will be forthcoming. If the agency itself records the interview, ask for a copy of the tape. If the interviewer takes notes, they should be typed up and gaps filled in as soon as possible after the interview is completed, so that the information is preserved while it is fresh. The team leader should promptly receive a copy of the transcript of each interview and should share its results with other investigators.

While investigators obviously should not be rude, they should not be timid, either. As citizens, they have a right to know what their government is doing and if government officials are abusive or uncooperative the investigator should not hesitate to assert his rights. If there is not a local "right to know" or "freedom of information" law comparable to the federal law guaranteeing citizen access to government information, and if the agency refuses to cooperate, then the investigation must become an adversary process. Information about the agency's uncooperativeness should be released to the press, and a plea for help should be made to agency employees who may be prepared to blow the whistle and release information on their own. The study group's phone number and post office box should be released, so conscientious employees who wish to cooperate to stop corruption, secrecy, waste, or lawlessness, despite official opposition, can reach the investigators.

In addition to interviewing present agency personnel, valuable information can be gleaned by interviewing former employees of the agency, people who do business with the agency, and those who used to do business with it. Because these people are removed from the agency's jurisdiction, there is a greater chance to receive information other than the straight "party line." Also, former employees who left unhappily are often willing to criticize the agency more freely. Be sure, however, to check the accuracy of such people's statements; they may be bearing personal grudges.

The interviewing process can be extended indefinitely— there is always one more person who can be talked to. But at some point it must end and the final report prepared. The report should be readable, interesting, and as complete as possible. Every assertion of fact should have data backing it up. If a piece of information is of doubtful veracity, it should not be included in the final report. One or two mistakes in an otherwise perfect 200-page report will be loudly pointed out by the agency and will serve to discredit the entire report in the eyes of skeptical observers. If the report is incomplete because of the size of the study, lack of time, or lack of cooperation by agency personnel, it should be labeled preliminary and other organizations or legislative committees should be urged to continue the study.

The style of writing in the report is important. Dry, technical data may be interesting to a scholar, but most laymen will not bother to wade through it. Therefore, the writing style should be lively and the report liberally spiced with case studies that name names and illustrate the report's main conclusions. If the report is long, a summary should be prepared for the press. If the findings are controversial, a press conference should be held at which the investigative team is present to answer reporters' questions.

Recommendations for specific reforms are essential in a study of this sort. These can be included in the final report, but they should also be advocated after the report is issued. Government hearings are an excellent forum for reemphasizing the report's findings and helping to build the popular support needed to bring about reforms. If the government does not call hearings, the study group can convene a citizens panel to hold its own hearings (see page 179 for information regarding citizen hearings).

Universities can become the base of operations for a continuing series of investigative probes, based on this model. Seminars can be organized around a specific agency probe or a continuing monitoring project. A term's course work can become an investigation of a local government agency, with the professor acting as team leader and the class divided into task forces for the study.

A citizen probe of government, in and of itself, cannot bring about major reform. But it can be the first step in an important process to open government to the people. Information is power and the information obtained through the detailed study of an agency's policies can provide materials for the larger effort to restore responsiveness to government.

How to Improve
Small Claims Courts

A small claims court is a court of justice with simplified procedures, no requirement for a lawyer, and an upper limit to the dollar amount that can be awarded in judgments. Courts with other names—conciliation courts, J.P. courts, magistrate's courts—sometimes also fit this definition. A small claims court can be an important target for citizen action. If it is functioning as it should, it can be a cheap, effective means of redress for a wide variety of people, from the TV owner cheated by the local repairman to the car owner who wants to sue Chrysler Corporation. Small claims courts are local courts, and most of the action for public information and reform can take place at the community level, supplemented in certain cases by action in state legislatures. At a time when inflated legal fees make having an attorney in a civil case a luxury that most people cannot afford, small claims courts can give the average citizen access to the law without the expense of a lawyer.

The overall goal of small claims reform is to create a situation in which citizens are aware of the existence of small claims courts and their potential uses, in which such courts are *easily* available in all communities, and in which these courts provide an inexpensive, convenient, effective forum for citizens. A second general purpose of research on these courts is to pinpoint problems in the community which may be revealed by a pattern of repeat appearances in the court records: landlords who repeatedly withhold security deposits, irresponsible towing companies, furniture stores with exploitative credit practices, and many others. Each court will have a slightly different story to tell.

Small claims courts are so underutilized that they may even be difficult to locate. Calling the civil division of your nearest local courthouse may get the answer; small claims courts are often just a separate session of the municipal or district court, using the same judges and facilities. Remember that the name of the court may vary from place to place. The sheriff's office or police station may know where justices of the peace have their courts. In desperation, call the office of the state attorney general. In some cases, however, there will not be anything like a small claims court available; about 41 million Americans, by our estimate, have no small claims court. In these cases, write the Small Claims Study Group whose address is listed at the end of this section. If your district does have a small claims court you should find out how it operates.

Interview. Start with the clerk. Find out from the clerk how the system is supposed to work, who uses the courts, etc. Then check what the clerk says against the statutes and against what others say. Talk to judges, other officials, local lawyers involved with the courts or with legal aid activities. Most important, talk to the people who find themselves in the court as plaintiffs or defendants.

Examine court records. These are public information. If you are denied access to them, this fact in itself deserves to be made an issue. Remember, small claims records will tell you the outcome of hearings, but they will usually not tell you whether victorious plaintiffs ever collected their money, an important point. So you will have to extract the names and addresses of a sample of such plaintiffs from the records and contact them by phone or mail. From our experience, you will be successful with one out of every eight names.

Court-watching. Go to the sessions. Remember to find out who the judge is. If lawyers are allowed, do they throw their weight around? Do litigants seem confused about what's going on? Does the judge explain his decisions? How much time is spent on each case? What is the general atmosphere—legalistic or informal? You will think of other questions.

Public information surveys. Try to find out how many people in the community know about the court, how much they know, and how they found out (from lawyers and inside sources, or through public sources like the media). Don't ask "Have you heard of small claims court?" Instead, present a situation for the respondent to remedy, asking, for example, "Suppose your landlord refused to return your security deposit. What would you do?"

A BRIEF CHECKLIST TO EVALUATE YOUR LOCAL SMALL CLAIMS COURT

1. What is the level of public awareness of the court?
2. Is there in your community any regular, on-going program designed to inform the public about the courts?
3. Are the courts actually informal and non-technical, or do most people in fact need lawyers to represent them? (If they need lawyers most of the time, you're back on square one: it's not a small claims court.)
4. Can the court be easily located?
5. Is an adequate manual or guidebook (not just a two-page publicity brochure) available to all litigants free of

charge? Are copies available in appropriate foreign languages?

6. Are at least half the sessions held in the evenings or on Saturdays?

7. Are lay advocates (not lawyers, but given some training) available to help citizen-litigants?

8. Is the dollar limit of jurisdiction *at least* $800? (A lower limit prohibits too many actions.)

9. Are lawyers permitted, and are their actions curtailed in any way? (Most authorities argue that small claims courts are no place for lawyers.)

10. Is the average hearing date less than three weeks from the time the case is filed?

11. A. Can collection be made against a corporation unwilling to pay a judgment? B. Are provisions for such a collection action simple, able to be carried out by a layman acting with little assistance? C. How often do individuals suing corporations win their cases? How often do they collect their judgments?

12. Are volunteer arbitrators available to supplement the work of the judges?

13. What is the average amount charged by lawyers for appearing in court?

14. Do court procedures provide for inquests? How careful is the examination given to collection claims brought by businesses when the defendant does not appear (defaults)?

15. Have clerks and judges received any special education in recent developments in consumer law?

16. What are the most frequent kinds of cases brought?

17. What percent of the total cases are collection claims brought by businesses?

18. Do litigants feel they get a fair chance to say their piece?

19. Is there a system of appeal or removal to a higher court? Is it used by landlords and businesses as a delaying tactic rather than a way to get a jury trial?

20. Do members of local minority groups use the court in proportion to their numbers in the local population?

Many other problems and patterns will occur to you during your investigation. As we suggested above, court records can lead you to a number of other problems, like the need for laws regulating rent security deposits, particular businesses who abuse credit procedures, or the need for a restructuring of legal fees.

The small claims court is the only place where a citizen can haul a major corporation into court and make it pay. It is probably the only place where the individual citizen, regardless of his race or poverty, stands on an equal footing with commerce.

Depending on what your investigation turns up (and there is no small claims court in existence which can't use improvement), release the results of your research with a statement about the need for a change in the courts. You may want to call for public hearings or a citizen conference. If the investigation of the small claims court reveals a need for legislation, seek allies such as the League of Women Voters in getting them corrected. One useful technique with small claims court legislation is to contrast the weaknesses of the existing court with courts in other states. For example, the New York City court at Harlem is considered by many a model court: evening sessions, volunteer arbitrators, lay advocates, inquests, a non-technical atmosphere, help for Spanish-speaking litigants, etc.

You can get further help from the sources and resources listed below:

Small Claims Study Group, Quincy House, Room 1, Cambridge, Mass. 02138. Tel: 617–491–8006. (Information on allies in your state, latest developments, literature, etc.)

The Harlem Model Court: Narcissus Copeland, Community Advocate at the court, 212–369–8811; John Howland, NYC Department of Consumer Affairs, 212–566–1694.

Western Massachusetts Public Interest Research Group, 233 N. Pleasant Street, Amherst, Mass. 01002. (Handbook on how to use small claims courts, $0.25.)

"Buyer vs. Seller in Small Claims Court," *Consumer Reports* (October 1971), Consumers Union, 256 Washington Street, Mount Vernon, N.Y. 10550.

"Small Claims Courts: Reform Revisited," 5 *Columbia Journal of Law and Social Problems* 47 (1969).

VI

FASHIONING
THE TOOLS
OF CITIZENSHIP

The preceding chapters have outlined many areas where citizens can be active to better their lives and their society. Some of the projects are easier than others. Some can be accomplished by a few people working informally together; others require organizations and even a full-time staff. Obviously, not every person has the opportunity, the desire, or the skill to devote full-time to the practice of citizenship. But the practice of citizenship does not require the full-time devotion of all persons. The volunteer, able to contribute only a few hours in the evening or one day a week, can investigate television repairmen, track down employment discriminators, and demand that his or her doctor prescribe generic drugs. What a difference it would make if a fraction of the time now spent watching football on television were spent watching for sex discrimination on television!

Every worker, too, has the opportunity to be an on-the-job public citizen. The housewife on her shopping rounds can gather data for retail price comparisons and begin to demand top nutritional and economic value for her dollar.

On-the-job public citizenship demands seeing that health and safety laws are obeyed, income reporting requirements are met, and environmental controls are adequate. When a plant dumps its wastes into the river by night or "cleans up" its air pollution by bleaching its smoke, when a store grinds rotten meat into sausage, or when a government agency suppresses information, the individuals working within each institution often know exactly what is happening. The remarkable fact about the Pentagon Papers was not that Daniel Ellsberg revealed their contents, but that so many people remained silent for so long.*

Nevertheless, there is a critical need for men and women who will devote all of their energies to working for consumer and environmental protection, honest government, equal opportunity, and similar causes. Without the full-time public citizen, the effectiveness of the volunteer and the on-the-job public citizen is diminished. Without at least one full-time worker, part-time efforts can too easily become diffuse or break down altogether. Yet the number of full-time public citizens need not be large. Eight people in Connecticut, working under the auspices of the Connecticut Citizen Action Group, became the focal point for significant citizen initiatives. Less than three dozen researchers working with Ralph Nader have issued fifteen major reports, filed over twenty lawsuits, and participated in innumerable government hearings. A few dozen full-time public citizens in each state, aided and supported by volunteers and on-the-job public citizens, can begin to tip the balance away from vested interests to the public interest. The organizations

---

* On-the-job public citizenship can have its risks, too; employees should usually try to persuade their employers to correct bad practices before blowing the whistle publicly. For more information on employee rights and for guidelines as to when and how to blow the whistle, see *Whistle Blowing* by Ralph Nader, Peter Petkas, and Kate Blackwell (Grossman, 1972). Potential whistle blowers should also contact the Clearinghouse for Professional Responsibility, P.O. Box 486, Washington, D.C. 20036. All inquiries will be kept strictly confidential.

that support citizen action can be formal or informal, heavily funded or run on a shoestring. Some have a single mission, such as consumer protection, environmental preservation, better housing, or equal employment opportunity. Others may focus on several areas simultaneously or on several issues within a broad area. Each type serves a particular purpose, and communities must determine which model is best for them. In areas where a single issue is of paramount importance—such as water pollution in a fishing village, transportation in a town threatened by major highway construction, or property taxes in a locality where a reassessment has raised rates 100 or 200 percent—a single-issue group may be most suitable. A single focus may also be appropriate if the constituency of the group has a common identity—women, blacks, motorists, boat owners, or homeowners. On the other hand, a multi-issue group can appeal to a broader constituency, and, in the long run, may outlast the one-issue organization.

There are two basic types of citizen action organizations. One is chartered, funded, employs a full-time staff, and operates on a citywide, statewide, or regional basis. The other is made up of volunteers, functions more informally, and usually confines its projects to a more limited area, such as a neighborhood or a town. For clarity, we shall refer to the former as a Citizen Action Group and to the latter as a Citizen Action Club.

The Citizen Action Club

To form a Citizen Action Group requires a substantial commitment by the initial organizers of time, energy, and, in some instances, money. Not every citizen activist is capable of making such a large effort, nor is every community able to marshal enough resources. A Citizen Action Club is an alternative.

A Citizen Action Club is an organization of concerned citizens joined together to better the community in which they live. Other organizations, of course, are set up for the same general purpose—they may raise money for charity, give scholarships, or perform other worthwhile services. A Citizen Action Club operates in a different area. Its tools are investigations, exposés, appearances before governmental bodies, lawsuits, and other responsible tactics to accomplish its purpose. It deals with replacing unjust power with just power.

Often Citizen Action Clubs are ad hoc, single-issue organizations formed to accomplish a specific goal. They may be set up to lobby for a law, to reform a town's property taxes, to establish a community daycare center, to oppose a utility rate increase, or to halt construction of a nuclear power plant nearby. Many of these activities are controversial. The community-wide acclaim bestowed on a Rotary Club that raises scholarship money or a Kiwanis that donates toys to an orphange will rarely be given to a Citizen Action Club. The factory owner who finds his privileged tax arrangement a matter of public knowledge is not going to enroll as a club booster. Nor will the druggist who reads in the paper that his prices are the highest in town. A Citizen Action Club performs a watchdog function and activists should be warned that success may bring acclaim, but it is also likely to produce some enemies as well.

A Citizen Action Club must focus on issues, undertaking projects within the community. To be successful, it must be action-oriented, its image lean and hard. Social gatherings, discount programs, charter flights, and other activities which bind other clubs together will probably be absent in the Citizen Action Club. Instead, members should devote their energies to a single issue area and be given responsibility for carrying out a specific project.

Successful clubs usually begin by working on an issue which affects its members directly—such as health care availability, fair tax assessments, or town or municipal services. The initial projects should be small, specific, and achievable. Later, when the club gains strength and experience, more ambitious efforts can be launched.

If the club is working on a single project, the project team itself can handle all club activities. As activities expand, some members have to be willing to assume greater responsibility. But it is important to guard against creeping bureaucracy. Our experience shows that most clubs can function adequately with the following tasks apportioned among individuals on the basis of talent, availability, or interest.

Club Coordinator. The coordinator keeps financial records, maintains club files, arranges meetings when necessary, and in general, oversees the activities of the group. If the club has several projects underway simultaneously, the position of coordinator obviously assumes greater importance.

Press Relations. An individual with some writing experience and knowledge of the media should be assigned to handle press relations. Media access may be the strongest asset a Citizen Action Club possesses.

Project Director. Each project should have a director who is well-informed about the issue at hand and able to organize the activities of others effectively to meet deadlines. If the club has only a single project underway, this responsibility can be handled by the coordinator.

Legal Specialist. Since many of the club's activities involve interpretation of laws, it is important to have at least one member familiar with legal research. Ideally, this person should be a lawyer, but since volunteer lawyers are not always easy to find, a law student or even a lay person willing to plow through legal jargon is sufficient in some instances.

Unlike the effort to form a Citizen Action Group, a minimal budget is needed by a citizen club. If homes are used instead of offices and if volunteers supply the personnel, most other expenses can be taken care of by a dues assessment, small enough that no one will find it burdensome. If additional funds are needed, they can be raised by an ad hoc money collection or by special events such as those described in the section on funding a Citizen Action Group. In time, if the club achieves recognition and membership grows, the services of a full-time coordinator may be needed.

Specialized Citizen Action Groups

Intermediate in size and scope between a Citizen Action Club and a full-fledged Citizen Action Group, are special-interest professional groups that are uniquely suited to tackle special problems. Fishermen, for example, are a natural lobby for strict water pollution control, because pollution directly threatens their livelihood; they are also in a unique position to observe sources of pollution. Truck drivers have a similar stake in safe vehicles and a similar ability to watch for safety hazards. Teachers, whose salaries are increasingly pinched by the so-called taxpayers' revolt, are personally affected by property tax inequities and by wasteful government projects that compete with education for the tax dollar.

Such special-interest groups can organize themselves expeditiously into public-interest activists. By focusing on the issues that most directly affect their own lives, they may also accomplish a great deal for the betterment of the community at large. These groups can launch projects like those suggested for broad-based citizen action groups. Or they can very easily provide a funding base for the support of lawyers, scientists, or other appropriate professionals who will work full-time in their interest. In this way, the technical resources and expertise of public-interest professionals can be combined with the financial resources and local knowledge of those who have a particular stake in a given issue.

Individuals with a common interest band together and raise money either by contribution, fund-raising events or both; proceeds of the funding effort are then pooled and administered by an elected board which represents the group. The board hires a professional staff and sets the priorities for action. The professional staff works on its own and with citizen volunteers to implement the board's priorities and directives. Members of the organization providing the funding base can be as involved in the actual projects as their time or interest permits. The important thing is that they will have established a source of on-going financial support for professionals who are then free to work in the public interest unhampered by institutional restraints or constrictions.

This strategy has been followed promisingly by several constituency groups. Sport and commercial fishermen's associations have combined under the banner of the Fisherman's Clean Water Action Project (P.O. Box 19312, Washington, D.C. 20036) to fund teams of scientists and lawyers who have the skills to combat water pollution. Frequently, resort and boat owners, scuba and surfing clubs, and individuals who depend on resort trade join the fisherman, broadening the coalition's base. The resulting effort combines the talents of these concerned volunteers with the on-going efforts of the professional staff.

Truck drivers who feel abandoned by their union when it comes to issues of health and safety have followed a similar strategy. Contributing twenty dollars dues per year, more than four hundred drivers have joined The Professional Drivers Council for Saftey and Health (PROD), P.O. Box 69, Washington, D.C. 20044. PROD's legal and medical consultants offer advice and assistance to drivers and serve as a watchdog on the Department of Transportation. Members of the organization collect information and complaints from their fellow drivers and forward them to the Washington staff. In this way, a data base is built up and recurring hazards or defect patterns can be spotted.

The American Automobile Association and Savings and Loan Association projects described in the consumer section of this manual offer opportunities for constituency group campaigns. Large PTAs, state associations of women's clubs, commuter organizations, credit unions, recreational or travel clubs, union locals, and dozens of other similar groups can be mobilized to protect their own and the public interest in this way. The most successful of these efforts so far is a student effort, the PIRG program.

How to Mobilize Student Activism: The PIRG Program

Student activism has come a long way from that day in February, 1960, when four Bible-carrying black students sat down at a lunch counter in North Carolina and refused to move until served. They and the thousands of white and black civil rights workers who followed their example ushered in a decade of campus concern with issues such as peace, ecology, and women's rights. But, student activism is plagued by recurring problems. More than most citizens, students' lives suffer from gaping discontinuities. The school year is divided into terms, and terms are further subdivided by holidays, classes, and examination periods. Activities follow the academic cycle. Campus-led voter registration drives, tutorial programs for the poor, or environmental projects usually collapse in June. This lack of continuity has prevented students from building on-going movements. Lack of expertise can also hamper student efforts when problems are not readily susceptible to solution simply by symbolic demonstrations, marches, or sit-ins.

To provide expertise and continuity, many students in various parts of the country have organized their own citizen action groups. They call these organizations PIRGs, Public Interest Research Groups. The first PIRGs were formed in Oregon and Minnesota during the 1970–71 academic year. PIRGs are now active in fourteen states and the movement is spreading rapidly. Over 400,000 students are involved.

Although new, PIRGs have already begun to make their presence felt. Even a partial list of their accomplishments is impressive. The Minnesota PIRG successfully halted timbering by the Forest Service and five lumber companies in the Boundary Water Canoe Area along the United States –Canada border; to require police to wear visible identification badges at all times while on duty; to permit nineteen-year-olds not only to vote in Minnesota but to run for office; and to require the Republican and Democratic parties to comply with the laws and publish the locations and times of precinct caucus meetings. MPIRG has also prepared a handbook on tenant rights in Minnesota, and prepared reports and studies on subjects as diverse as discrimination against women by Minneapolis employment agencies, snowmobiles, the hearing aid industry in Minnesota, and the state clean air plan. During its first year of operation, MPIRG's fourteen-person staff worked on more than sixty separate projects.

OSPIRG, the Oregon Student PIRG, is funded by students at twelve Oregon campuses. OSPIRG recently conducted a major study of advertising fraud in the Portland area which uncovered widespread use of illegal "bait and switch" tactics. Thorough critiques of a proposed mass transit system for Portland resulted in the city's plan being scrapped and a new proposal drawn up along the lines suggested by OSPIRG. OSPIRG also has issued reports on procedures setting utility rates, water pollution in the Willamette River and Coos Bay, the effects of clear-cutting practices on Oregon's forest reserves; and on discrimination against women who attempt to obtain credit from banks and other institutions. Thirty-two courses are being offered on nine Oregon college campuses in which students can receive academic credit for OSPIRG-related research.

The Vermont PIRG has issued studies on conflicts of interest among Blue Cross directors, the impact of the ski industry on Vermont, and the effects of new highway construction around Burlington. VPIRG sponsored a statewide conference on Vermont health care, and has formed a statewide citizen lobby with offices at the state capital in Montpelier. VPIRG staff have testified before legislative committees on the Equal Rights Amendment and health care, and have urged broader interpretations of the Vermont "right to know" law.

In New Jersey, the PIRG spearheaded a successful fight to defeat a $650 million transportation bond that provided funds for highways and largely ignored mass transit needs. NJPIRG is supervising over one hundred students on ten research projects.

The Western Massachusetts PIRG has filed a major law suit to overturn allegedly unfair state procedures for setting utility rates. The attorney general has filed an *amicus* brief joining the PIRG suit, and the case is pending before a three-judge federal court in Boston. WMPIRG has issued the study on prescription drug prices mentioned in chapter II, and has drafted and will lobby for laws regarding the posting of prescription drug prices and for the free substitution of generic equivalents in place of higher-priced brand name drugs.

The Missouri PIRG drafted a new consumer code to protect poor people in St. Louis and has produced and distributed a model lease for use by tenants. MOPIRG also participated in a study of the Educational Testing Service and is working with St. Louis area unions to secure better enforcement of the occupational safety and health laws.

The Texas PIRG issued a major study of the Austin Capital Improvement Plan, pointing out its weaknesses. Voters subsequently turned down a bond issue to finance the plan. Its investigation of drug prices was discussed in chapter II.

PIRGIM, the PIRG in Michigan, uncovered an old law imposing criminal sanctions on landlords for gross housing-code violations. PIRGIM presently is suing to have this law enforced.

PIRGs are set up in the same way as many other student activities. Students on a campus hold a referendum or petition to join a PIRG. Elections are held to select students to sit on a local board of directors to manage the campus program. Once elected, the local board selects members to sit on a state board composed of representatives from all participating schools. These students hire the professional staff and set policy for the group. The money to pay for salaries and expenses comes from the student activity fee, which usually amounts to only three or four dollars a year from each student.

Each PIRG operates as an independent nonprofit, non-partisan tax-exempt corporation. No formal ties exist between PIRGs and each group is kept wholly separate from the universities, which serve as collecting agents for the activity fee.

Organizing a PIRG requires three steps.* First, the student body at large must approve the idea. Once students have approved the program, trustees or regents must give their O.K. President Edward Bloustein of Rutgers echoes the words of many administrators who support the PIRG concept: "Activities like skiing and chess clubs are funded out of student fees. They have less of an integral relation to education than this [PIRG]."

Once a professional staff is hired, the PIRG is ready to begin tackling problems of general public concern. Staff and students work together. Students, through their elected representatives, set broad policy guidelines and do much of

* A complete guide to PIRG organizing is spelled out in *Action for A Change: A Student's Manual for Public Interest Organizing* by Ralph Nader and Donald Ross (Grossman, 1972).

the background research. The staff and interested faculty members supervise student investigators and, when the data is collected, professionals carry out the major part of the action program. Depending on the particular case, "action" may consist of publication of an exposé, drafting a new law or regulation, lobbying, or litigation.

The success of the PIRG program on the campus should serve as a model for high school students and other citizen groups. Credit unions, fraternal associations, professional societies, unions, and numerous other groups can utilize this same model to form their own groups.

How to Form a
Citizen Action Group

The largest, most ambitious, and potentially most effective form of public citizen action is the full-fledged Citizen Action Group, employing a professional staff and acting on behalf of the public interest on many issues. There are three ways such a group can be formed. It might grow naturally out of an existing network of citizen action clubs and specialized citizen groups. The smaller groups could continue to work on their own, while providing a constituency, direction, and financial support to the larger organization.

If not enough clubs exist, or if they are unwilling to band together, a Citizen Action Group will have to be built from scratch. There are two ways to form it. If the organizers of the group can raise enough money from foundations and wealthy individuals to support a small full-time staff, it can get down to work immediately and save the development of a citizen constituency until later when it is a proven instrument. The alternative is to form the citizen constituency first by conducting a fund-raising drive among the people; once the money is raised, the group can hire staff, get to work, and solidify its support by its success.

Each of these three approaches has advantages and disadvantages. To build from a base of existing clubs creates an automatic constituency, but the Citizen Action Group also risks bogging down in debates on priorities, methods, goals, and jealousies among clubs. An environmental group might not want to work on sex discrimination until the factory upriver is investigated for pollution; a property tax organization might feel that county governments should be investigated before state governments.

Citizen action groups that begin with start-up money from foundations and wealthy individuals can start work immediately, which makes later appeals to hire people for funds easier because the group has proven its reliability and success. On the other hand, a group with no popular constituency might find it hard to influence legislators. Most important, large private grants normally are given only to citizen groups that qualify as nonprofit, tax-deductible entities. This status does make fund-raising easier since donors, particularly those in the upper-income brackets, can deduct a portion of their gifts from their federal tax return. But it also limits the group's activities. To any substantial extent, a tax-deductible group cannot lobby or organize other citizens to lobby. A further limitation is that such grants seldom are made unless the action group staff has impressive credentials.

Attempting to raise funds from large numbers of citizens before undertaking action projects is very difficult unless the organizers have a reputation for integrity and effectiveness or unless the idea is so powerful that citizens naturally support it. On the other hand, if successful, it develops a constituency extremely loyal to the new organization. This constituency is a source of continuing support and potential volunteer workers. Small contributions from large numbers of citizens leave the group without any obligations, actual or implied, to a few large contributors. Further, a mass base, especially in the form of dues-paying members, offers more stability than single-source support. Foundations are fickle and important programs may lose their funding because they no longer are fashionable.

Finally, while a tax-deductible status is critical for most large donors, it is relatively unimportant to small givers. The deduction available even to those in the highest tax brackets on a contribution of less than $100 is insignificant.* If possible, therefore, a Citizen Action Group should ignore the short-run benefits of deductibility and choose instead a nonprofit status that permits lobbying and all forms of citizen organizing. An intermediate position would be to form two separate groups, a deductible one to receive large grants and a nondeductible one that can lobby freely. Tax laws permit this arrangement, but a lawyer familiar with the subtleties of the tax code should be consulted as to details.

The emphasis in this section is on the last of these strategies. This choice is dictated by three facts. First, building a coalition of existing groups to form a Citizen Action Group is a task that cannot easily be reduced to written procedures. The political and interpersonal factors will vary in every case. Second, obtaining foundation grants is not practical for the vast majority of groups. Moreover, it is our experience that those who can qualify usually know how to apply and so directions are superfluous. Third, raising funds from a large constituency is an alternative many activists have never considered. Although difficult, it can be accomplished without a preexisting base of support and without substantial start-up funds. Thus, it offers the greatest flexibility.

* A full discussion of various tax statuses available to citizen groups may be found in chapter 7 of *Action for a Change*.

PHILOSOPHY

The philosophy underlying the concept of a Citizen Action Group is quite simple. Time and time again decisions affecting vital public interests are made by a few people in isolation without regard for the total impact of their decisions on public well-being. Special interests, particularly big business and some big labor unions, are almost always represented by skilled lawyers, lobbyists, and public relations specialists. But who represents the public? Government regulatory agencies are too often understaffed, underfinanced, poorly informed, or have become the political prisoners of the economic interests they are supposed to watch over. Many legislators routinely endorse the conduct of the agencies they are supposed to scrutinize, spend most of their time running for reelection, or owe political debts to powerful campaign contributors. Others attempt to carry out their duties but are frustrated by the structure of the legislature, lack of staff, or lack of interest on the part of their fellow legislators.

To right the balance and to restore an open system which takes multiple opinions into account, skilled citizen advocates are needed. A Citizen Action Group can supply this expertise on a continuous basis. What distinguishes a Citizen Action Group from numerous existing citizen groups is its staff, a combination of full-time professionals—lawyers, economists, scientists, doctors, and organizers—backed by volunteer and on-the-job public citizens. It is not an educational or recreational organization. Rather it is a well-honed instrument for change.

Though the need for citizen advocacy is apparent, establishing a strong Citizen Action Group can be difficult. One reason is that citizen activists are often so troubled by the issues that they attempt to work on them before the group is organized. They may achieve some initial success, but often, and particularly if the issue is large, they are overwhelmed by the work or worn down by lack of resources. The following organizing plan does not pretend to be all-inclusive. In every effort unexpected problems arise and there are always loose ends. However, the techniques outlined below are models which can be duplicated or adapted to meet varying circumstances. A more detailed discussion of organizing techniques is contained in chapter 5 of *Action For A Change*.

STAGE 1: PLANNING THE CAMPAIGN

From its inception, it is important that the organizing effort have both broad representation and a clear purpose. If the group is to be citywide or statewide, each neighborhood in the case of the former and each population center in the case of the latter should be represented. If the group is to appeal to a single constituency, all factions of the constituency should be represented equitably. For example, if support from college students is sought, fraternity and nonfraternity, dormitory and commuter students should be represented. If a citywide organization is being formed, representatives from rich and poor areas, racial and ethnic minorities and from other citizen groups should be invited. Cliquishness, snobbishness, and exclusivity will erode an organizing effort. The absence of a clear purpose will halt it almost as quickly. Therefore, it is essential that the goals of the group be well-defined from the outset.

Great care should be taken to line up allies and to avoid offending other groups with similar interests. It often seems that the only things some environmental and consumer groups dislike more than pollution or fraud in the marketplace are other environmental and consumer groups. Citizen resources are too few and too precious to be squandered on rivalries among groups that should be allies.

Financing

The initial money to pay for the printing of brochures, posters, solicitation letters, or foundation proposals that will be used to solicit larger amounts of financing can in most cases be raised by the organizers themselves with small personal contributions.

More difficult than raising start-up money is obtaining permanent support. By their nature, programs that set out to effect change are likely to lurch along from financial crisis to financial crisis. The broad public acceptance which makes fund-raising a relatively easier matter for organizations like the Community Chest or the United Fund is unavailable to a group whose mission is to act as a prod on the status quo. Consequently, organizers of a Citizen Action Group must recognize from the outset that regardless of their source of support, it will probably be relatively unstable.

Establishing a membership organization is one way of building mass support on a continuing basis. Membership implies more than a one-time-only contribution. Because members have a stake in the outcome of the group's projects, they are a good source of volunteer workers. Special fund-raising events, of course, can supplement the income from members.

Membership, however, is a mixed blessing, especially if the group is large. If care is not exercised the paraphernalia that often accompanies membership—newsletters, cards, special mailings, renewals, meetings, etc.—may overwhelm the citizen group. Another problem is that unless the group is structured in such a way that rapid decisions can be made and executed, many important issues may be lost. Also, one or two members intent on protecting a special interest may hinder action in that area. The choice of whether or not to form a membership group is a matter for local decision. If membership is ruled out, it is still possible to enroll people as "supporters," "contributors," or "donors" to the group.

Dues from "members" or "supporters" can be collected annually, quarterly, or monthly. The latter is the preferable method despite the attendant increase in bookkeeping. Most people are not in a position to pay more than ten or twenty dollars in a lump sum to support a citizen group no matter how worthy its purpose. But many of these same people can contribute three, four, or five dollars a month even though it adds up to more money annually. Working with low-income consumers, chapters of CEPA (Consumer Education and Protection Association) supports itself in this way. CEPA chapters are organized along community lines, but larger organizations have been funded this way. Several political candidates in 1972 used predated monthly checks as a means of raising funds.

Every state, even the smallest, is sure to have at least 4,000 people sufficiently committed to the concept of responsible citizen action to be willing to contribute a monthly donation of four or five dollars. And if this method proves unsuitable an annual fee of $10.00 from several thousand activists can go a long way toward funding a group's activities. In addition, special arrangements can be made for those who cannot afford this sum.

Timetable

Generally, the fall and spring are the best times to launch citizen organizing efforts. The Chistmas season and the summer months are the worst possible times to hold a drive. The actual length of the public portion of the campaign will depend on both the scope of the effort and its purpose. It should last from ten to fifteen weeks, starting slowly and building gradually to a climatic week or two of money collecting.

Once a schedule is fixed, it should be adhered to. Even if the funding goal is not achieved by the final deadline, the campaign should be stopped unless there is solid evidence that momentum is still building. To allow a drive to linger on until it peters out from exhaustion or boredom is destructive of the entire effort. It is better to raise a little less and to end the campaign on a rising note of strength.

Summation

By the end of the planning stage, several important issues must be resolved. First, the strategy for the fund-raising campaign should be clearly mapped out; second, individual responsibilities for carrying out the campaign must be understood; and third, sufficient resources for implementing the initial drive must be in hand. The exact sum of money needed will depend on such variables as the size of the effort, the amount of free supplies donated, the number of allied groups supporting the effort, and the receptivity of the community. All literature, posters, and other materials needed during the campaign should be prepared, and the office of the secretary of state, mayor, or city manager should be contacted to make sure that the proposed fund-raising drive is legal—a license is usually required to solicit money for a charity. Finally, all interpersonal disputes between organizers must be resolved before the campaign moves from the planning stage to public action. Nothing is more destructive to an effort than internal bickering or petty vendettas. If a person cannot work with other organizers or has irreconcilable differences about the conduct of the campaign or the future of the group, that person should be asked to resign before the effort goes public.

STAGE 2: THE CAMPAIGN

If the proper groundwork has been done during the planning stage, the actual campaign should run smoothly. The first steps are to set up a central office and to select personnel for each of the key posts. The next task is to do the same for each local neighborhood post. An office must be located, equipment and supplies obtained, phone service installed, bank accounts opened and access to mimeograph facilities assured. This phase of the operation can take a week or two.

The best way to recruit workers is to announce the campaign as soon as the central office has been established. If the campaign is to be statewide, it should be launched with a press conference at the state Capitol. An appeal for volunteers made during the press conference should render a sufficient number of workers.

The central office should coordinate the overall drive, which might be organized out of regional offices, which are in turn further subdivided into town, neighborhood, and school committees. The advantage of this structure is that each office is accountable for the performance of the drive in its own area. In addition, it permits local people who know the area best to tailor the drive to their own particular circumstances. Finally, separate offices tend to reduce dissension and to isolate it when it does occur. Even if one office out of five ceases to function effectively because of internal or external reasons, the campaign can still proceed successfully.

The state office and each local office should have at least four people in positions of administrative responsibility: the coordinator, publicity director, treasurer, and organizer. The state office coordinator is the person in charge of the entire campaign, to whom each local coordinator is directly responsible. Coordinators should be good administrators with some public-speaking experience. The stronger and more resourceful the local coordinator, the less the state office has to involve itself in that region's campaign.

This elaborate apparatus is set up to do three things simultaneously: organize and run the volunteer network, spread word of the new group's existence, and raise funds. The fund-raising effort is largely dependent on the success of the other two.

Publicity

Without expensive paid advertisements, the only way to gain media recognition is by qualifying for public service time or by generating news. All radio and television stations are obliged to donate a certain amount of air time to public service broadcasting. Not every station will agree that a Citizen Action Group qualifies as a public service. But a citizen group that prepares a short statement of purpose or an announcement of a coming event can usually persuade some radio stations to broadcast it several times a day as a community service. If station management becomes convinced that the group is worthwhile, they may be willing to endorse the campaign editorially.

To get additional newspaper coverage or broadcast media time, news has to be generated. The definition of what constitutes "news" varies. In smaller towns, a speech before the local Rotary Club may receive front-page coverage, while in large cities, it takes a major event to obtain recognition. If the campaign is being organized by existing clubs, they may be able to release information, reports on charges in the name of the new group.

Posters, leaflets, and brochures describing the purposes and goals of the group can also be distributed to attract attention. Most of these can be prepared during the planning stage. They need not be elaborate, although in a sense their quality will reflect on that of the entire campaign.

Another way to attract favorable coverage is to have effective speakers address service clubs, community organizations, church groups, and school assemblies. This can help to spread word of the group's existence, and to give it a personal impetus. A good speaker can be immensely important in recruiting new workers and securing the support of new allies for the fund-raising campaign.

Fund-raising

Be forewarned that until the group has proved its worth and built up a following, it will be difficult to attract dues-paying "members" or "supporters." One way to hurdle this gap between beginning a Citizens Action Group and scoring the successes needed to recruit a sustaining member-ship is to undertake a series of fund-raising projects to raise enough money to sustain the group during its first six to twelve months.

The best fund-raising events are those that require little advance preparation, publicity, or expense and that can be repeated time and again by people not under the direct supervision of campaign coordinators. Although individually these events are small and bring in limited sums of money, in the aggregate they can be quite significant. Events which fall into this category are bake sales, car washes, auctions, cocktail or wine-tasting parties, and assorted other events such as raffles and dances.

More difficult to coordinate, but more remunerative, are major events such as concerts, door-to-door or shopping center solicitations, film showings, button sales, and marches for money. All but the last are familiar and need no ex-planation. A march for money is a fairly recent phenomenon that has been used to raise money for Biafran refugees, UNESCO, and hospital drives. The formula is simply for several hundred or several thousand students to solicit neighbors, friends, and local businesses in order to obtain sponsorship at a rate of $1 or $2 a mile for each mile of a five-, ten-, or twenty-mile march. Again, except for tickets and some publicity, advance expenses can be kept minimal. The proceeds, however, can be gigantic. A march of ten miles by 1,000 people at a $1 a person per mile can raise $10,000!

It should be obvious that a determined citizens group can organize a campaign, attract workers, and raise money if the idea is sufficiently exciting and the organizers are tough enough to repeat endlessly the message that average people acting in concert can create a force strong enough to change the quality of life in a community or even an entire state. It is an effort that requires great stamina and a high degree of motivation. It also requires coordination. But it can be done and done successfully.

STAGE 3: FORMATION OF THE GROUP

With funds collected, the group is ready to begin operations—after a few procedural steps have been taken. The organizing committee should either be formalized as a board of directors, or if the group is a membership organization, elections should be held to select directors. Once the direction of the group is legitimatized the next step is to hire staff.

Professional staff should be relatively easy to find, since there is an increasing demand by young professionals to harmonize their values with their employment. Such people are willing to make major financial sacrifices and to work long hours in less than plush conditions to perform jobs that are personally satisfying. Even before the fund-raising campaign is over, applications for permanent staff positions are likely to be flowing in. The staff director should be recruited first so that he or she can participate in selecting other staff. Ideally, the staff director should have previous administrative experience, knowledge of the city or state and legal, organizational, or research skills. The core of the professional staff should be lawyers. Lawyers are essential because often the solutions to complex problems are found in the courts, in executive agencies, or in new legislation. Moreover, their training gives them sufficient versatility to move from one problem area to another and integrate the skills of the remaining staff members such as scientists, economists, or community organizers who should be recruited according to need.

Once a staff has been hired, care must be taken to use both professional and financial resources wisely and effectively. Energies should be expended on high-leverage projects, aimed at making an enduring impact. Too many citizen groups waste their resources on low-impact projects. The environmental activities of many campus-based ecology clubs are a good illustration of this problem. Instead of using their library, laboratory, or class projects to work on important environmental problems, these groups typically have talented researchers wandering around dormitory halls collecting newspapers for recycling. Not that there is anything intrinsically wrong with recycling. But it is a drop-in-the-bucket measure. If solid-waste disposal is the issue of the moment, a campus ecology club would do better to organize a campaign to convince the school to collect papers, cans, and glass. Or if the group has a larger focus, to persuade a nearby town or city to take over the problem. Or pressure for laws to require the companies to use more ecologically appropriate packaging or containers for recycling, and the like. Cost-benefit analyses, feasibility studies, model ordinances followed by a lobbying campaign are higher-leverage projects by which a school group can achieve maximum impact and perpetuate a recycling campaign after the first group of eco-activists has graduated.

The same is true for nonstudent groups. Litter clean-up campaigns or green recycling bins in shopping centers are at best symbolic gestures, good for awareness development. At worst, they are excuses for not taking more decisive action. It is almost always a mistake to attempt, on a long-term basis, to provide a service such as litter clean-up or recycling, which our municipal government is supposed to perform. Citizen groups have neither the resources nor the staying power to take on this kind of project. When they try, the end result can be disillusionment and cynicism. There are generally far more productive ways for a citizens group to use its available resources. The Connecticut

Citizen Action Group provides an excellent example of an effective, high-leverage citizen organization.

CONNECTICUT CITIZEN ACTION GROUP: A MODEL

The Connecticut Citizen Action Group (CCAG) was formed during the spring of 1971 by scores of Connecticut volunteers aided by a national organizer from Ralph Nader's office. The initial three-month organizing period from February to May was devoted primarily to fund-raising, with a simultaneous effort to establish public recognition of the group's existence.

During the first ten weeks of the campaign, only a few thousand dollars were collected, but the climactic last week brought in approximately $35,000 in donations. Money was solicited in a variety of ways from many different groups, but the strongest response came from money marches by high school students. The largest march attracted 3,500 participants, while several smaller marches had crowds in the hundreds. By June, the $5,000 of seed money that had been collected at the beginning had swollen to $52,000. And although there was no initial membership drive, the group has started a subscription program to enroll dues-paying members, as part of its second-year funding drive.

The next step, after fund-raising, was to hire a director. In late June, Toby Moffett, a twenty-seven-year-old with experience as director of the Office of Students and Youth in HEW was hired. By September, a full-time staff of eight was employed, an office was equipped, and the group was ready to begin work.

During the next ten months CCAG had a major impact on the life of Connecticut. It is no exaggeration to say that the CCAG staff, with an average age of twenty-five, average salaries of $4,000 per year, and an average work week of over sixty hours per person, transformed the notion of citizen representation in Connecticut.

The most significant CCAG project was the formation of a 3,000-member Citizens Lobby, which provided a powerful mechanism by which citizens could express their views immediately and forcefully on a variety of issues affecting their welfare. The lobby operated in the following way.

Each lobbyist was tied into the main CCAG office by means of a telephone link-up. The main office would call forty regional coordinators around the state, informing them that a particular measure was coming to a vote. They in turn would contact twenty-five people within their own telephone exchange. These thousand citizens would each call three to five other people to bring the lobby up to full strength. The response of lobbyists in the form of letters, phone calls, and telegrams would be registered with a public official or an agency over the next four- or five-day period. In a state the size of Connecticut, a reaction of two or three thousand citizens to a proposed policy, either in favor or against, is likely to have an important impact on state policy.

There are many other CCAG projects in addition to the Citizens Lobby, a brief enumeration of which will indicate the scope of their program:

—A property tax investigation of Wallingford, Connecticut;

—Publication of a property tax handbook for citizens;

—Intervention in a telephone rate case contesting an increase in intrastate rates;

—Investigation and exposure of manufacturing defects in the M-16 rifle (the Justice Department and the FBI at present are deciding whether to bring charges against Colt's executives);

—Participation at all levels, including at hearings around the state, in the preparation of clean air emission standards for Connecticut;

—Disclosure of conflicts of interest in the governor's appointments to a utility council;

—A full-scale, 1200-page report on state legislators;

—Preparation of an environmental platform for the state of Connecticut;

—Opening and maintenance of the Connecticut Buyer's Action Center and the Hartford Automobile Complaint Center.

CCAG is the forerunner that proves the concept that citizen advocacy by aggressive, full-time public citizens backed by hundreds of part-time volunteers can have a significant impact on state affairs. And on a $52,000 first year budget—about the salary of one Madison Avenue advertising executive—at that!

CCAG wisely did not get trapped into low-leverage activities. Rather, they used their resources to monitor and prod government into doing what it was supposed to do but wasn't doing. When they did propose a governmental function, such as preparation of clean air standards, their aim was to set an example and then to hold government to it.

The Connecticut group chose its staff wisely, selecting the most highly motivated applicants. They did not rush to the newspapers with each tidbit of information they uncovered. Instead, they carefully built a citizen lobby and established personal contact with reporters and other citizen groups around the state. They thus attained a reputation for hard work and resounding accuracy. Only then did they "go to the public" with their case. When they did, their attack was sharp and its immediate effect was, for example, the resignation of two officials whose conflicts of interest they had exposed publicly. At the end of a year of this kind of hard-hitting activity, CCAG had emerged as the strongest citizen organization within the state of Connecticut and a model for other citizen action groups around the country.

A Final Word

The few projects contained in this first edition by no means exhaust the possibilities open to creative and responsible citizen activists. Most of them are modeled on the work of individuals or organizations associated with Ralph Nader. We hope to widen our focus in the future, with new editions of *A Public Citizen's Action Manual.*

To do this we need your help. We'd like to know whether you find these projects helpful, whether another format would prove more useful, where you think improvements can be made. If you or an organization to which you belong undertakes one of these projects, we would be most interested in a report on its outcome along with press clippings or other information.

Finally, in the next edition of this manual we'd like to include projects designed by public citizens operating on the state or local level. Please send us suggestions for new projects that you think would be helpful to other citizens. We cannot promise to acknowledge each new idea or to include each one in the next book, but you can be sure that we will consider each suggestion carefully.

Donald Ross
Citizen Action Group
2000 P Street, N.W.
Washington, D.C. 20036